WITHDRAWN

Lecture Notes
in Economics and
Mathematical Systems

Operations Research, Computer Science, Social Science

Edited by M. Beckmann, Providence, G. Goos, Karlsruhe, and
H. P. Künzi, Zürich

69

S. Ashour

Sequencing Theory

Springer-Verlag
Berlin · Heidelberg · New York 1972

Advisory Board

H. Albach · A. V. Balakrishnan · F. Ferschl · R. E. Kalman · W. Krelle · G. Seegmüller
N. Wirth

Prof. Dr. Said Ashour
Iowa State University
Ames, Iowa 50010, USA

AMS Subject Classifications (1970): 90 B 35

TS
157.5
A82

ISBN 3-540-05877-X Springer-Verlag Berlin · Heidelberg · New York
ISBN 0-387-05877-X Springer-Verlag New York · Heidelberg · Berlin

This work is subject to copyright. All rights are reserved, whether the whole or part of the material is concerned, specifically those of translation, reprinting, re-use of illustrations, broadcasting, reproduction by photocopying machine or similar means, and storage in data banks.

Under § 54 of the German Copyright Law where copies are made for other than private use, a fee is payable to the publisher, the amount of the fee to be determined by agreement with the publisher.

© by Springer-Verlag Berlin · Heidelberg 1972. Library of Congress Catalog Card Number 72-83014. Printed in Germany.

Offsetdruck: Julius Beltz, Hemsbach/Bergstr.

PREFACE

The intent of these notes is to provide an appreciation of sequencing theory, and to develop an awareness of the combinatorial aspects of sequencing problems. An understanding of the ideas and concepts presented in these notes will provide the necessary background to enable further study in this rapidly growing subject. These notes have been used as a part of one-semester courses in Operations Research for both senior and first-year graduate students.

Following the introductory chapter, several classes of scheduling models are discussed in Chapter 2. Chapter 3 is devoted to discussing the characteristics of several types of criteria that have been proposed in the literature. Because of the importance of the combinatorial properties in the analysis of scheduling models, various combinatorial aspects are treated in Chapter 4. The primary objective of such a treatment is to provide the reader with an insight into the nature of the problem. Due to the tremendous number of sequences involved, and the fact that many sequences have the same schedule time, statistical sampling has elicited a great deal of theoretical studies. Two such studies, one of which has evolved from my research, are reported in Chapter 5. Many references to basic sources are cited at the end of each chapter to provide a guide for further readings.

I am indebted to Professor Santa Arora of the University of Minnesota who introduced me to the subject during my graduate career. I have been extremely fortunate in receiving valuable comments and constructive criticism on an early draft of the manuscript from Professor Salah E. Elmaghraby of North Carolina State University at Raleigh. These notes have been prepared at Kansas State University, and I gratefully acknowledge the support and encouragement received. Special thanks are due to my graduate student Prakash Bhatt for proofreading the first draft. Further, I wish to express my deep appreciation to Marie Jirak for her skillful typing of several drafts of these notes and to Janet Athavichitchanyaraks, Leslie Fletcher, and Jan Gaines for excellent typing of the final manuscript. Finally, and most importantly, I am grateful to my wife for her patience and encouragement during the writing of this manuscript.

March 1972   Said Ashour

TABLE OF CONTENTS

CHAPTER 1: INTRODUCTION 1

CHAPTER 2: BASIC STRUCTURE 5
    2.1 Problem Definition 5
    2.2 Problem Formulation 12
    2.3 Problem Assumptions 29

CHAPTER 3: MEASURES OF PERFORMANCE 34
    3.1 Characteristics of Criteria 34
    3.2 Single Criteria 39
    3.3 Multiple Criteria 56

CHAPTER 4: COMBINATORIAL ASPECTS 65
    4.1 Characteristics of Sequences 65
    4.2 Characteristics of Schedules 88

CHAPTER 5: STATISTICAL ASPECTS 109
    5.1 Theoretical Study I 109
    5.2 Theoretical Study II 116

CHAPTER 1

INTRODUCTION

A shop production system, in which a wide variety of jobs are handled according to customer specifications, is traditionally found in jobbing-type machine shops. The complex behavior of the machine shop, which consists of several work centers each of which has one or more machines of the same type, can be described as follows.

The work in the machine shop is usually initiated by receiving orders from customers. The order may comprise one or more jobs, each of which should be engineered before being released to the shop. This includes: (1) establishing the technological ordering in which the job is to be processed on the machines; (2) specifying the materials, fixtures and tools which are required to perform the job; (3) determining the economical batch size, if any, in which the job is to be processed; (4) estimating the processing time, including job transportation, and machine setup times, if any, for each of the operations comprising the job; and (5) setting the time limit by which the job should be completed in response to a delivery date dictated by the customer, or for inventory replenishment. When the job is released to the shop, it is then routed through the work centers to perform the associated operations. Each of these operations takes place at one and only one work center. It is natural that any job may comprise a number of units which may be determined on an economical batch size basis, or specified in the customer order.

In scheduling a set of jobs through the shop, the objective is to ensure that the prescribed technological ordering of each job is satisfied, and there are no conflicts between jobs while attempting to meet job due-dates or other criteria. The ideal situation in such a shop is that machines are kept continuously busy, manpower is just sufficient to handle the work load, materials and in-waiting inventories, and end-product inventory, if any, are kept at reasonable levels, and job due-dates are set that they can be met. In practice, however, the shop usually accommodates itself to the current situations regardless of scheduling procedures or rules. Indeed, as Pounds [6] has pointed out, it is possible for shop management not to be aware of the existence of any scheduling problem because the other components of the total shop production system have acted to shield management from strongly interdependent scheduling problems.

The majority of academic research on shop scheduling has centered on the sequencing problem. The sequencing problem is concerned with determining the sequence in which a set of jobs is to be performed on each of a number of machines. This problem is, of course, only a part of the overall production control problem in a shop production system. The sequencing problem is preceded by the planning area which involves the functions of material procurement, technological processes, productive capacity, routing requirements, processing time estimates, and shop loading. On the other hand, the sequencing problem is followed by the control area which involves the regulations and adjustment of production activities to conform to plans Because of the strong interaction between the sequencing problem and its preceding and succeeding areas, it is not immediately obvious how one can either isolate the sequencing problem or assess precisely the impact of sequencing decisions on the other decisions, and vice versa. In fact, the areas of capacity planning, shop loading, and job sequencing are strongly interrelated to the extent that decisions in one area do strongly influence decisions in the other two.

Although the most interesting production control problems arise in the totality of the capacity planning, shop loading, and job sequencing areas; the sequencing theory itself is worth studying for several reasons stated by Elmaghraby [3].

> First, a meaningful study of a multi-stage system such as the more common production system necessitates intimate knowledge of each component. The sequencing phase is one such component, and its detailed study is therefore an essential element of the study of the complete system.
>
> Second, the advent of the computer as an operational tool for the management of productive systems tends to eliminate a great deal of the "fat" previously found in these systems. This, in turn, emphasizes the effect of hitherto secondary decisions, such as those concerned with sequencing.
>
> Third, continued and expanded education in operations research and management sciences is beginning to bear fruit in the form of improved management information systems. This has led to great strides in the other aspects of the production function, such as inventory, loading, financing, and so on. Further improvement in some of these areas is, in fact, constrained by the possible improvement in the sequencing area.
>
> From a pedagogical point of view,..., sequencing theory is an excellent demonstration of the applicability of several theoretical models (such as linear programming and mathematical abstractions (such

as combinatorial analysis) to everyday problems. It has proved invaluable in rendering these conceptual formulations understandable to the students.

Traditional scheduling procedures are typically designed to cope with the complexities of shop scheduling, where each job is unique and no prescribed technological ordering exists. These procedures depend on graphical devices such as Gantt chart or its concepts to help maintain control of the shop operations. The Gantt chart, an innovation of the scientific management era, has been developed by Henry Gantt. A complete discussion of the basic Gantt charts has been presented by Clark [1]. Essentially, a Gantt chart is a device for portraying the information regarding the progress of each job in the shop and the current capacity of machines. It also pinpoints potential and actual problems in time for corrective action to be taken. Although Gantt charts are useful in developing feasible schedules, they are not, of course, a substitute for decision making. Scheduling decisions include, for example, the time at which a job should be released to the shop, and the sequence in which the jobs should be performed on each machine to meet one or more measures of performance.

Until 1954 there has been virtually no reported attempt to treat the shop scheduling problem analytically with the explicit purpose of optimizing some measure of performance. Since that time, however, the study of the shop scheduling problem and its contexts has attracted researchers from every field. This is due to the development of operations research techniques and their application to an area previously dominated by intuition and judgment; and due to the increased awareness of management to the potential gains realizable when good scheduling practices are employed. Theoretical models representing simple shop scheduling problems have been formulated and analyzed utilizing operations research techniques such as combinatorial analysis, dynamic programming, integer programming, reliable heuristics, and network analysis approaches. The principal difficulty with these approaches, however, has been that the computational effort required increases rapidly even with a relatively small size problems and simplified assumptions. Shop scheduling problems have been formulated as queueing models. However, due to the difficulty in solving such models analytically, various groups have pursued the study of shop scheduling problems utilizing computer simulation techniques. Several references in which excellent expositions on possible approaches to shop scheduling problems, are cited below.

REFERENCES

[1] Clark, W., *The Gantt Chart: A Working Tool of Management*, Sir Isaac Pitman & Sons Ltd., London, England, 1952.

[2] Conway, R. W., W. L. Maxwell and L. W. Miller, *Theory of Scheduling*, Addison-Wesley Publishing Company, Reading, Massachusetts, 1967.

[3] Elmaghraby, S., "The Machine Sequencing Problem - Review and Extension," *Naval Research Logistics Quarterly*, Vol. 15, No. 2, 1968, pp. 205-232.

[4] Mellor, P., "A Review of Job Shop Scheduling," *Operational Research Quarterly*, Vol. 17, No. 2, 1966, pp. 161-171.

[5] Muth, J. F., and G. L. Thompson, eds., *Industrial Scheduling*, Prentice-Hall, Inc., Englewood Cliffs, New Jersey, 1963.

[6] Pounds, W. F., "The Scheduling Environment," Chapter 1 in *Industrial Scheduling*, (eds. J. F. Muth and G. L. Thompson), Prentic-Hall, Inc., Englewood Cliffs, New Jersey, 1963.

[7] Sisson, R. L., "Methods of Sequencing in Job Shops - A Review," *Operations Research*, Vol. 7, No. 1, 1959, pp. 10-29.

[8] Sisson, R. L., "Sequencing Theory," Chapter 7 in *Progress in Operations Research*, (ed. R. M. Ackhoff), John Wiley & Sons, New York, N.Y., 1961.

[9] Spinner, A. H., "Sequencing Theory - Development to Date," *Naval Research Logistics Quarterly*, Vol. 15, No. 2, 1968, pp. 319-330.

[10] Thompson, G. L., "Recent Developments in the Job-Shop Scheduling Problems," *Naval Research Logistics Quarterly*, Vol. 7, No. 4, 1960, pp. 585-589.

CHAPTER 2

BASIC STRUCTURE

Different scheduling problems naturally lead to different models. In this chapter we shall discuss several classes of these models. In order to provide an insight into the structure of the problem, we shall introduce an explicit mathematical formulation which can be represented by Gantt chart, and a linear graph. Finally, several assumptions restricting the analytical models, which have been developed to date, will be discussed.

2.1 Problem Definition

The classical shop scheduling process may be characterized in terms of the following context. A machine shop is equipped with various groups of machines. Each machine group consists of a number of identical machines with respect to their ability to process the expected work in the shop. The amount of work constitutes several jobs to be performed on the machines. Each job may consist of a single unit or a batch of identical units, usually determined on an economical basis. Any job requires one or more operations, each of which is to be processed on a single machine. An operation is determined entirely by the specification of the job and the machine involved. The operations comprising each job are processed on the machines in a specified routing, hereafter referred to as a machine ordering. The machine orderings are usually imposed by technological requirements which always dictate the basic manufacturing process and types of machines, fixtures and tools to be used.

Associated with each operation is a processing time which is required for the complete performance of this operation. The processing time of an operation may consist of: (1) the job transportation time--the time required to transport the job from one machine to another according to the prespecified machine ordering; (2) the machine setup time--the time required to prepare the machine for performing that operation; (3) the operation running time--the time required to perform the job on a particular machine; and (4) the machine teardown time--the time required to reset the machine after the operation has been completed. As the jobs flow through the shop, the associated operations must compete with one another for each of the machines, due to the limited capacity of the available machines. When all operations comprising a job are completed, the job departs from the shop as a completed job.

Although the shop scheduling problem is demonstrated in the manufacturing contexts, it arises quite naturally in almost all areas of endeavor such as hospital, school, bank, and government. The pervasive nature of shop scheduling problems can be illustrated by considering the following operational systems:

1. the scheduling of cars (jobs) to be serviced for a limited number of mechanics (machines) in a car repair shop.
2. the scheduling of classes (jobs) to classrooms (machines) in an academic institution.
3. the scheduling of patients (jobs) on a limited number of test equipments (machines) in a hospital.
4. the scheduling of ships (jobs) on a limited number of berths (machines) in a harbor.
5. the scheduling of shipments (jobs) on a limited number of trucks (machines) in a loading dock.

Many other operational systems which can be structured as a single-machine system encompasses realistic situations. For example, the scheduling of programs (jobs) to be run on the computer (single-machine) in a computing and data processing center, and the scheduling of cities (jobs) to be visited by a salesman (single-machine), the well-known traveling salesman problem.

As a consequence of the above description, the shop scheduling problem arises whenever it is necessary to schedule a set of jobs on a number of machines in a specified machine ordering, so that the sequence of these jobs is optimal with respect to a given measure of performance. The effectiveness of performance of the shop may be measured in terms of one or more criteria such as minimum cost, minimum in-waiting inventory, minimum completion time of all jobs, maximum profit, maximum utilization of machines and manpower, or ability of meeting job due-dates, whichever is or are most appropriate. A study of the criteria usually involved in shop scheduling problems will be carried out in the succeeding chapter.

There has been a lack of standardized terms in the area of shop scheduling. Therefore, it seems appropriate to define a number of basic terms. This will fix the fundamental concepts for the mathematical formulation and the analysis of the shop scheduling problem. The basic terms with their definitons are:

<u>Job</u>. A job is a unit of a product or a batch of identical units, that must be processed on certain machines. An alternative name is a task, commodity, lot, job lot, production lot, production run, or shop order.

<u>Machine</u>. A machine is a single device capable of performing a certain process. An alternative name is a facility, processor, or work center.

<u>Operation</u>. An operation is an elemental task to be performed on a job by a particular machine. An operation is specified entirely by the job and the machine involved. An alternative name is a task, or activity.

<u>Processing time</u>. A processing time is the length of time which is required for the completion of an operation on a particular machine. It may include the time for setting up the machine, the time for transporting the associated job from one machine to another, and/or the time for tearing down the machine after operation. An alternative name is an operation time, of running time. The processing times for all operations may be combined in a matrix referred to as a processing time matrix.

<u>Machine ordering</u>. A machine ordering is an arrangement of a set of machines through which a particular job is to be performed, depending primarily on the technological requirements. The machine ordering of a job is usually described by the precedence relations of its operations. An alternative name is a routing, ordering, or technological ordering. The machine orderings of all jobs may be combined in a matrix referred to as a machine ordering matrix.

<u>Job sequencing</u>. A job sequencing is an arrangement of a set of jobs to be processed on a single machine. The job sequencing on a machine is usually described by the precedence relations between a set of jobs on that machine. The job sequencings for all machines may be combined in a matrix referred to as a job sequencing matrix.

<u>Sequence</u>. A sequence is a set of job sequencings, each of which is assigned to each of the machines. The sequence usually specifies the arrangement of the

operations comprising all jobs on all machines. Thus, a sequence can be simply represented by a job sequencing matrix. A sequence does not provide the time at which the operations are performed nor the existence of idle times between various operations. A feasible sequence is a sequence which is consistent with the prescribed machine ordering matrix.

Schedule. A schedule is a feasible sequence in which the starting and completion times of the operations comprising all jobs on each of the machines, are specified. It also specifies the idle time, if any, between the processing times of each two successive operations.

The amount of confusion resulting from various interpretations of the terms "sequencing" and "scheduling" is apparent in the literature. However, we shall provide suitable definitions to draw a distinction between both terms. Sequencing is concerned with the arrangements and permutations in which a set of jobs under consideration are performed on all machines. Scheduling is concerned with the specifications of the starting or completion times of certain jobs on all machines. Sequencing decisions focus on the arrangement of events; whereas, scheduling decisions focus on the time of events. The terms sequencing and scheduling, though distinguishable as above, are used frequently as synonyms. The reason for the frequent use of both terms interchangeably is that since it is always assumed that each job is started as early as possible, a schedule is automatically created when a particular sequence is sought.

As we attempt to structure the shop scheduling problem, a variety of situations encountered in operational systems dictates the types of scheduling models. For purposes of analysis, however, shop scheduling models may be distinguished by one or more of the following:

1. a single-machine process versus a multi-machine process.
2. a unique flow pattern for each job versus an identical flow pattern for all jobs.
3. a fixed finite number of jobs to be performed on various machines versus jobs arriving at the shop in a continuous fashion.

4. a complete and known information relative to jobs and machines versus one or more of the elements involved behaving in a probalistic manner.

In the first class of models, the number of machines in the shop provides the distinction between single-machine and multi-machine problems. Single-machine problems may seem to be trival or elementary for thorough analysis; however, their study is meaningful because there exists many operational systems of practical value in which a single-machine is involved. As an example, an oil refinery produces many different grades and classes of petroleum products. Also there is always a hope that any results in the single-machine case may lead to new avenues of possible investigations in the multi-machine case. It should be pointed out, however, that any results which hold for the multi-machine problem is also applicable to the single-machine case.

In the second class of models, the characteristics of job flow pattern in a multi-machine process provide the distinction between flow-shop and job-shop problems. Each job in a job-shop has a different flow pattern, that is, no common pattern of flow from machine to machine exists. However, in a flow-shop there exists a single flow pattern in such a way that all jobs flow from one end of the shop to the other. Thus machines can be thought of as existing in series. In such a shop the machines are numbered in ascending order starting from one end of the shop by machine 1 and ending by machine M, where M is the total number of machines in the shop. As an example, in a certain flow-shop all jobs may move from shearing, to pressing, to machining, to grinding, and end with polishing.

Although flow-shops resemble assembly-lines in that all jobs have identical flow pattern, they differ in many ways. First a flow-shop is equipped to handle a variety of jobs, as opposed to a standard product performed on an assembly-line. Second, the jobs in a flow-shop do not have to be processed on all machines. In other words, a job may skip one or more operations according to its engineering content. However, all jobs on an assembly-line have to move from one work station to another. Third, in a flow-shop each machine is independent of the others and can be scheduled separately; whereas, each work station on an assembly-line depends on the preceding one. Fourth, each job has its own processing time at each machine in a flow-shop; however, all the units of a product have a standard performance time at each work station on an assembly-line. As might be expected, the flow-shop problem may be considered as a special case of the job-shop problem, and thus its analysis may be simpler. In general, this is not the case as will be discussed in Chapter 4.

In the third class of models, the behavior of job arrivals at the shop provides the distinction between static and dynamic problems. In a static problem a fixed finite number of jobs arrive simultaneously at the shop and are immediately available to be performed on a number of idle machines. Thus the static problem does not explicitly take the variable time into consideration. On the other hand, in a dynamic problem jobs are arriving intermittently at the shop. Thus the dynamic problem deals with the variable time.

The static problem is, in itself, a drastic simplification of the realistic shop process. Analytical solutions thus far obtained for this problem are restricted to very simple cases and thus have a little practical value. However, as Nugent [12] has pointed out, the static problem is of interest as a prelude to the dynamic problem because it provides a way to treat the dynamic problem as a series of static problems. Experiences gained through the analysis of the static problem would undoubtedly help us understand and gain insight to the solution of the dynamic problem. Although the dynamic problem is that which is usually faced in the actual shop process and is, therefore, of more intrinsic interest, the static problem is not without inherent interest of its own. This is because the static problem arises in various realistic situations. For example, a certain number of cars (jobs) having an 8 AM appointment arrive on time at a car repair shop. These cars which have been engineered previously by service management, must be completed by 5 PM of the same day. Various repairmen (machines) with various capabilities and specialities are available. It is desirable to determine a schedule that specifies the time at which each car is to be performed by each repairman. Furthermore, the static problem is interesting as a special class of combinatorial problems, the methods of analysis for which should be applicable to other combinatorial problems such as traveling salesman, delivery, and line-balancing problems.

In the fourth class of models, the behavior of the elements comprising the basic structure of the problem provides the distinction between deterministic and stochastic problems. The deterministic models are characterized by the fact that these elements do not involve chance variation and that the consequences of any given decision can be predicted in a precise manner. The stochastic models, however, are characterized by their explicit recognition of chance variations and uncertainty which could exist in one or more of these elements. In such a case, the elements which vary stochastically, are assumed to be predictable only in a statistical sense.

The elements included as a substance of the problem, which may or may not behave in a probabilistic manner, are as follows: (1) the characteristics of the jobs which include the behavior of job arrivals to the shop, the job due-dates, if any, and the relative importance of each job; (2) the engineering requirements of each job which include the number of operations, the machine ordering, the processing times, and other constraints, if any; and (3) the characteristics of the machines which include the number of machines, the available capacity of these machines, and the ability and suitability of each machine in performing the jobs.

The variety of situations that can be encountered in shop scheduling problems has been the object of considerable research efforts. Shop scheduling problems are analyzed by the application of sequencing and dispatching approaches. In the sequencing approach, a sequence of jobs for each machine is sought in advance. Thus, sequencing pertains to the process of specifying an arrangement of a set of jobs to be performed on each of the machines involved.

In the dispatching approach, on the other hand, dispatching rules are sought that can be applied at each machine to assign a job from among a number of jobs waiting to be performed. The selection of a dispatching rule must be made in the light of its effect on the operations in the shop. Examples of dispatching rules are as follows: (1) select the job on first-come, first-served basis; (2) select the job with the shortest processing time; and (3) select the job with the earliest due-date. Thus, dispatching pertains to the process of assigning a job to a particular machine according to some dispatching rule which is usually based on immediate or current shop information.

2.2 Problem Formulation

In the previous section we have defined the shop scheduling problem in its simplest form. In order to provide an insight into the structure of the problem, we shall present an explicit mathematical formulation as well as Gantt chart and linear graph representations.

In the discussion which follows we shall use some notation to help us express and deduce the properties of the precedence relations of the various operations. We shall designate a job by an index j and a machine by an index m. Since an operation is specified entirely by the specification of the job and the machine involved, such an operation will be represented by a pair of indices (jm).

The indexing of jobs and machines is arbitrary; it does not necessarily correspond to the sequence in which the jobs are performed on each machine or to the order in which the machines process each job. Since we may process the jobs on any machine m in some sequence other than the preconceived one, we shall designate the jobs as

$$j_1, j_2, \ldots, j_k, \ldots, j_J ,$$

where J is the total number of jobs. For example, a particular job j_k indicates the job index which is in the sequence-position k.

On the other hand, in considering a permutation of the machines for any job j with respect to the preconceived order, the machines will be designated as

$$m_1, m_2, \ldots, m_\ell, \ldots, m_M ,$$

where M is the total number of machines. For example, a particular machine, m_ℓ means the machine index which is in the order-position ℓ. In general, the subscripts for j and m are used to denote the position in a permutation sequence and permutation order, respectively.

Consequently, since it will be necessary to consider permutations of the job sequence on a particular machine, permutations of the machine order for a particular job, and even permutations of both the job sequence and the machine order, the following set of operations are defined. The operation of a particular job j_k on machine m is designated (j_km); the operation of job j on a particular machine m_ℓ is denoted (jm_ℓ); and a specific operation involving a particular job j_k and a particular machine m_ℓ is designated ($j_k m_\ell$).

In shop scheduling problems it is necessary to consider the order relation for each job to be performed through the various machines. The elements of such a relation are the operations to be scheduled. The basic order relation which connects these operations is usually referred to as a binary or precedence relation.

In order to define the precedence relation, consider three operations $(j_\pi m_\delta)$, $(j_u m_v)$, and $(j_\chi m_z)$. If the processing of job j_π on machine m_δ must start before the processing of job j_u on machine m_v, then operation $(j_\pi m_\delta)$ is said to precede operation $(j_u m_v)$. This precedence relation is designated

$$(j_\pi m_\delta) < (j_u m_v) ,$$

where $<$ indicates the precedence relation. It may also be said that operation $(j_u m_v)$ follows operation $(j_\pi m_\delta)$. The precedence relation has the following properties:

1. The precedence relation is transitive, that is, if

$$(j_\pi m_\delta) < (j_u m_v) \quad \text{and} \quad (j_u m_v) < (j_\chi m_z) ,$$

then

$$(j_\pi m_\delta) < (j_\chi m_z);$$

2. The precedence relation is non-reflexive, that is, there is no operation that precedes itself, or simply,

$$(j_\pi m_\delta) \not< (j_\pi m_\delta).$$

3. The precedence relation is non-symmetric, that is, if

$$(j_\pi m_\delta) < (j_u m_v) ,$$

then

$$(j_u m_v) \not< (j_\pi m_\delta) .$$

Next we define a particular subset of the precedence relation. Given two operations $(j_\pi m_\delta)$ and $(j_u m_v)$ having a job or a machine in common, that is, $j_\pi = j_u$ or $m_\delta = m_v$. The operation $(j_\pi m_\delta)$ is said to directly-precede operation $(j_u m_v)$, if there is no intermediary operations. Such a relation is designated

$$(j_\pi m_\delta) << (j_u m_v) ,$$

where $<<$ indicates the direct-precedence relation. It may also be said that operation $(j_u m_v)$ next-follows operation $(j_\pi m_\delta)$. This direct-precedence relation implies that

1. $(j_\tau m_\delta) \neq (j_u m_v)$,

2. $(j_\tau m_\delta) < (j_u m_v)$, and

3. there does not exist an operation $(j_\chi m_z)$ such that

$$(j_\tau m_\delta) < (j_\chi m_z) < (j_u m_v).$$

It should be noted that the direct-precedence relation is non-transitive. However, when this relation is extended to have the transitive property, it becomes a precedence relation.

Having defined the precedence and direct-precedence relations, the remainder of this section will be devoted to the mathematical statement and Gantt chart and linear graph representations of the shop scheduling problem.

Mathematical Statement

In scheduling problems, the direct-precedence relations are most often prescribed in advance because of the technological requirements. For example, a hole drilling operation must precede, or can directly-precede a tapping operation. In terms of the order relations defined earlier, the prescribed ordering of M machines for a job j, referred to as the machine ordering, may be arranged in a single chain of direct-precedences such that

$$(jm_1) \ll (jm_2) \ll \ldots \ll (jm_\ell) \ll \ldots \ll (jm_M).$$

The above machine ordering of a job j can be arranged in a row vector such that

$$M_j = (jm_1 \quad jm_2 \quad \ldots \quad jm_\ell \quad \ldots \quad jm_M), \quad j = 1, 2, \ldots, J.$$

The machine ordering M_j, is an ordered set of indices of the successive machines that perform job j. These sets of machine orderings, one for each job, may be combined in a (JxM) matrix called the machine ordering matrix and denoted by M. For example, consider a sample problem having two jobs to be processed on three machines. The orderings in which jobs 1 and 2 are performed on the three machines are such that

$$(11) \ll (13) \ll (12)$$

and

$$(23) \ll (21) \ll (22),$$

respectively. These machine orderings may also be written in row vectors such that

$$M_1 = \begin{pmatrix} 11 & 13 & 12 \end{pmatrix}$$

and

$$M_2 = \begin{pmatrix} 23 & 21 & 22 \end{pmatrix}.$$

As mentioned above, these machine orderings may be combined in the following machine ordering matrix:

$$M = \begin{pmatrix} M_1 \\ M_2 \end{pmatrix} = \begin{pmatrix} 1m_1 & 1m_2 & 1m_3 \\ 2m_1 & 2m_2 & 2m_3 \end{pmatrix} = \begin{pmatrix} 11 & 13 & 12 \\ 23 & 21 & 22 \end{pmatrix}$$

This matrix indicates that job 1 must be processed on machine 1 first, machine 3 second, and machine 2 last. However, job 2 must be performed on machine 3 first, machine 1 second, and machine 2 last. It should be noted that machine m_ℓ in the element $1m_\ell$ is not necessarily the same as machine m_ℓ in the element $2m_\ell$.

In a flow-shop in which all jobs have the same flow pattern, the machine ordering for job j can be expressed such that

$$M = \begin{pmatrix} j1 & j2 & \ldots & jm & \ldots & jM \end{pmatrix}, \qquad j = 1, 2, \ldots, J .$$

This indicates that job j is to be processed on machine 1 first, machine 2 second, ..., and machine M last. As mentioned in the preceding section, all jobs in such a shop, flow from one end of the shop to the other. The machines which can be thought of as existing in series, are numbered in ascending order from 1 to M along with the natural flow of all jobs in the shop. The subscript which indicates the machine order-position is, therefore, omitted. It should be pointed out that throughout this text, we shall not specify the machine ordering matrix for a flow-shop problem explicitly, since we shall assume that all jobs follow the above machine ordering.

Associated with each operation (jm_ℓ) there is a processing time t_{jm_ℓ}, that is, the time required to perform a job j on a particular machine m_ℓ. The processing times of each job on the various machines are usually estimated in advance. For convenience, the processing times corresponding to the machine ordering for a job j are designated

$$T_j = \begin{pmatrix} t_{jm_1} & t_{jm_2} & \ldots & t_{jm_\ell} & \ldots & t_{jm_M} \end{pmatrix}, \qquad j = 1, 2, \ldots, J.$$

The above sets of processing times, one for each job, may also be combined in a (JxM) matrix referred to as the processing time matrix and denoted by T. The processing time matrix of the sample problem is shown below:

$$T = \begin{pmatrix} T_1 \\ T_2 \end{pmatrix} = \begin{pmatrix} t_{1m_1} & t_{1m_2} & t_{1m_3} \\ t_{2m_1} & t_{2m_2} & t_{2m_3} \end{pmatrix} = \begin{pmatrix} t_{11} & t_{13} & t_{12} \\ t_{23} & t_{21} & t_{22} \end{pmatrix} = \begin{pmatrix} 2 & 4 & 1 \\ 3 & 4 & 5 \end{pmatrix}$$

The above processing time matrix indicates that to perform job 1 on machines 1, 3, and 2, it requires 2, 4, and 1 units of time, respectively. Similarly, job 2 requires 3, 4, and 5 units of time to be completed on machines 3, 1, and 2, respectively. It is obvious that if a job is not processed on a particular machine, a zero processing time can be placed in the corresponding element in the processing time matrix. In flow-shops, the processing times corresponding to the machine ordering for a job j are expressed such that

$$T_j = (t_{j1} \; t_{j2} \; \ldots \; t_{jm} \; \ldots \; t_{jM}), \quad j = 1, 2, \ldots, J.$$

While the machine ordering specifies the order in which a certain job is processed on various machines, the job sequencing specifies the sequence in which a certain machine performs a number of jobs. Using the definition of the direct-precedence relation, the sequencing of J jobs on a machine m, referred to as the job sequencing, may be arranged in a single chain of direct precedences such that

$$(j_1 m) \ll (j_2 m) \ll \ldots \ll (j_k m) \ll \ldots \ll (j_J m).$$

The above job sequencing on a machine m can be arranged in a row vector such that

$$J = (j_1 m \; j_2 m \ldots j_k m \ldots j_J m), \quad m = 1, 2, \ldots, M.$$

The job sequencing, J_m is an ordered set of indices of the successive jobs to be processed through a machine m. These sets of job sequencings, one for each machine, may be combined in an (MxJ) matrix called the job sequencing matrix and denoted by S. The job sequencing matrix is the sequence in which the various jobs may be processed on the machines. For example, one of the possible sequences obtained for our sample problem consists of the following job sequencings:

$$(11) \ll (21),$$
$$(22) \ll (12),$$

and

$$(23) \ll (13).$$

In terms of row vectors, the job sequencings are

$$J_1 = (11 \; 21),$$

$$J_2 = \begin{pmatrix} 22 & 12 \end{pmatrix},$$

and

$$J_3 = \begin{pmatrix} 23 & 13 \end{pmatrix}.$$

As mentioned above, these job sequencings are combined in the following matrix:

$$S = \begin{pmatrix} J_1 \\ J_2 \\ J_3 \end{pmatrix} = \begin{pmatrix} j_1^1 & j_2^1 \\ j_1^2 & j_2^2 \\ j_1^3 & j_2^3 \end{pmatrix} = \begin{pmatrix} 11 & 21 \\ 22 & 12 \\ 23 & 13 \end{pmatrix}.$$

This matrix indicates that machines 2 and 3 process jobs 1 and 2 in the sequence {2 1}; however, machine 1 performs the two jobs in the sequence {1 2}. In other words, machines 2 and 3 process job 2 first and job 1 second; and machine 1 processes job 1 first and job 2 second. It should be noted that job j_1 in the element j_1^1 may or may not be the same job in the elements j_1^2 or j_1^3. In the above matrix, the elements j_1^2 and j_1^3 have the same job which differs from that in j_1^1.

An examination of the machine ordering and job sequencing matrices reveals that the elements appear in S are the same as those in M. Consequently, the precedence relations in a certain sequence, represented by the job sequencing matrix, may not be consistent with those in the machine ordering matrix. Such a sequence is referred to as a non-feasible sequence. The concept of consistency will be discussed in chapter 4.

Most often the order in which each job is to be performed on a number of machines specified completely so that it remains only to determine the sequence in which the jobs are to be processed on each machine. Therefore, the static shop scheduling problem may be stated formally as: given both the machine ordering and processing time matrices M and T, it is required to find the optimal sequence S^* with respect to a certain measure of performance.

Gantt Chart Representation

A convenient way to represent a shop scheduling problem of J jobs and M machines is by Gantt chart. A Gantt chart is a horizontal bar graph with time scale, showing the activities of the operations involved. The activities of these operations may be depicted on a bar representing either a job or a machine as illustrated in Figure 2.1.

Gantt charts help demonstrate the interrelations and show the required coordinations of the various operations within the same job or the same machine.

Figure 2.1   Diagramatic Representations of a Machine Ordering of Job j and a Job Sequencing for Machine m

In the shop scheduling problem the combined requirements of the machine ordering and processing time matrices defined earlier may be represented by a Gantt chart. This chart is pictured as a set of a horizontal bars showing the starting and completion times of the successive operations comprising each job. Operation indices are marked inside the horizontal bar; and the numbers below each bar represent the starting and completion times of the various operations.

An example may elucidate the above discussion. Consider our sample problem which has been formulated previously. The combined requirements of the machine ordering and processing time matrices of this problem yield the Gantt chart shown in Figure 2.2. The first bar which represents job 1 shows that this job must be processed on machine 1 first, machine 3 second, and machine 2 last. One can see from this bar that machine 3 cannot be started on job 1 until the corresponding operation on machine 1 has been completed. Similarly, machine 2 cannot be started on the same job until the corresponding operation on machine 3 has been completed. Assuming that the time scale starts at zero, the completion times of job 1 on machines 1, 3, and 2 are 2, 7, and 8, respectively. Job 2 represented by the second bar in Figure 2.2, is performed on machine 3 first, machine 1 second, and machine 2 last. Considering that the time scale starts also at zero, the completion time of job 2 on all machines is 13.

The Gantt chart may be represented by matrices, referred to as Gantt matrices. For example, the Gantt matrix $G(M)$, shown below represents the Gantt charts appearing in Figure 2.2.

$$G(M) = \begin{pmatrix} 1 & 1 & - & 3 & 3 & 3 & 3 & 2 & - & - & - & - & - \\ 3 & 3 & 3 & 1 & 1 & 1 & 1 & - & 2 & 2 & 2 & 2 & 2 \end{pmatrix}$$

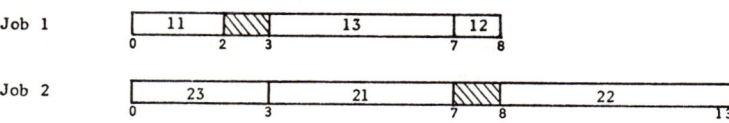

Figure 2.2 A Gantt Chart Depicting Machine Orderings

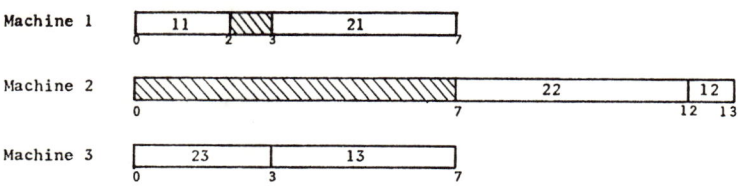

Figure 2.3 A Gantt Chart Depicting Job Sequencings

This matrix has as many rows as the number of bars, since each job is represented by a bar in the Gantt chart or a row in the Gantt matrix. Each element in $G(M)$ is either a machine index or a dash. If the element is a machine index, it indicates that a job j is processed on this machine during that unit of time. If it is a dash, it means that the job is waiting to be processed on the successive machine. Considering that the time is measured in discrete units, all processing and waiting times of a job are expressed as a multiple of this time which is equal to the processing time or waiting time, respectively. Since a machine cannot perform more than one job at the same time, the same machine index must not appear more than once in the same column in $G(M)$.

Using the above concept, the job sequencing matrix combined with the processing time matrix may also be represented by a Gantt chart. Figure 2.3 above illustrates the sequence S of our sample problem. This figure consists of three bars representing the three machines. For example, the first bar which represents machine 1 shows that this machine must perform job 1 first, and job 2 second. Considering the time scale starts at zero, the non-hatched portions in the bar indicate that machine 1 performs job 1 from zero to 2, and job 2 between 3 and 7. The hatched portion from 2 to 3 represents the machine idle time. Similarly, the processing of both jobs on machines 2 and 3 are represented by the second and third bars, respectively. It should be noted from this Gantt chart that the schedule time is 13 units of time, since it represents the completion time of the last operation.

The Gantt chart shown in Figure 2.3 may also be represented by the following Gantt matrix:

$$G(S) = \begin{pmatrix} 1 & 1 & - & 2 & 2 & 2 & 2 & - & - & - & - & - & - \\ - & - & - & - & - & - & - & 2 & 2 & 2 & 2 & 2 & 1 \\ 2 & 2 & 2 & 1 & 1 & 1 & 1 & - & - & - & - & - & - \end{pmatrix}$$

In this matrix, each machine is represented by a row; and each element is either a job index or a dash. For illustration, the first row can be described as machine 1 performs job 1 in 2 units of time, becomes idle for the next one unit of time, then processes job 2 in 4 units of time, and becomes idle again for 6 units of time. The fact that the same job index does not appear more than once in the same column in $G(S)$ satisfies the condition that a job cannot be processed on more than one machine at the same time.

It is of interest to illustrate the precedence and direct-precedence relations discussed earlier, by using the Gantt chart shown in Figure 2.4. For example, the direct-precedence relation

$$(j_1 3) << (j_2 3) \quad \text{or} \quad (23) << (13)$$

indicates that machine 3 performs jobs 2 and 1 consecutively. The precedence relations

$$(j_1 1) < (j_2 2) \quad \text{or} \quad (11) < (12),$$

and

$$(j_1 3) < (j_1 2) \quad \text{or} \quad (23) < (22),$$

hold. Since the operations in a set of precedences may be arranged in a single chain of direct-precedences, the precedence relation

$$(j_2 1) < (j_2 2) \quad \text{or} \quad (21) < (12)$$

consists of the following direct-precedences relations:

$$(j_2 1) << (j_1 2) << (j_2 2) \quad \text{or} \quad (21) << (22) << (12).$$

Note that in the direct-precedence relations, the operations must have the same job or the same machine.

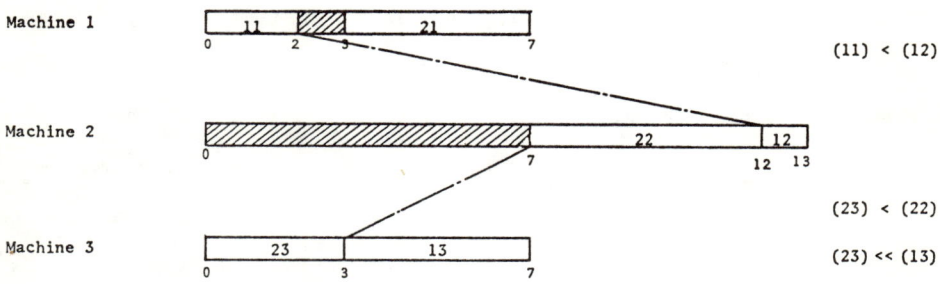

Figure 2.4 Precedence and Direct-Precedence Relations Illustrated by a Gantt Chart

Linear Graph Representation

The shop scheduling problem has been described and represented as a connected linear graph. Thus an applied problem such as the shop scheduling problem is brought within the highly developed mathematical discipline of graph theory. The theory of graphs consists of a rigorous definition of network structures and analyses of various problems. We shall briefly consider some of the fundamental notions of graph theory that are relevant to shop scheduling problems.

A linear graph $G(N; A)$ consists of a set of nodes $N = \{1, 2, \ldots, k, \ell, \ldots n\}$ and a set of arcs $A = \{(k, \ell)\}$. Nodes are sometimes referred to as points or vertices and arcs as links, edges, or branches. An arc is an ordered pair of nodes. The directed (or oriented) arc (k, ℓ) extends from node (k) to node (ℓ). A directed graph is one in which any node (ℓ) can be reached from any other node (k) through directed arcs in the graph. A directed chain between two nodes (k) and (ℓ) is a connected sequence of directed arcs that lead from node (k) to node (ℓ) such that each node is encountered only once. This implies that a chain contains forward arcs.

On the other hand, a path may contain forward as well as reverse arcs. In the context of the shop scheduling problem in which the existence of paths with reverse arcs is not permitted, we shall use path synonymously with a chain.

In describing the shop scheduling problem as a linear graph, each operation (jm) is represented by a node (k) of the graph, and the direct-precedence relations are pictured as directed arcs between pairs of nodes. The nodes corresponding to the operations are indexed such that node (k) = $j + (m-1)J$, where J is the total number of jobs. Associated with each arc (k,ℓ), there is a real number $t(k)$, representing the processing time of the operation corresponding to node (k). Consider our sample problem that we have been using, the nodes (1), (2), (3), (4), (5), and (6) correspond to operations (11), (21), (12), (22), (13), and (23), respectively.

Now we can construct a linear graph describing the direct-precedence relations of the machine ordering for each job. For example, the machine ordering matrix of our sample problem is depicted in directed linear graphs shown in Figure 2.5. Graphs 1 and 2 display the order of machines for jobs 1 and 2, respectively. It is also convenient to construct a linear graph describing a possible sequence. Such a sequence is constructed from the machine ordering graphs by connecting the nodes for each machine in a fashion which describes the sequence of the jobs through the machine. For example, Figure 2.6 shows the graph which represents the sequence S of our sample problem. Although it is convenient to display the starting time of each operation on the Gantt chart, it is not directly available on the graph. We shall, therefore, discuss a quasi-Boolean procedure for determining the starting time of each operation.

In examining the graph of Figure 2.6, it is apparent that, for example, node (1) precedes node (3), or simply, (1) < (3). There also exists two directed paths for reaching node (3) from node (1), namely, (1) << (5) << (3), and (1) << (2) << (4) << (3). The first directed path contains two direct-precedence relations: (1) << (5) and (5) << (3). Thus, it may be referred to as a two-level chain. In a similar manner, the second directed path may be called a three-level chain, since it contains three one-level chains. In general, the length of the directed path from one node to another depends on the number of one-level chains, that is, the number of direct-precedence relations. A directed path from a node to itself consists of a zero-level

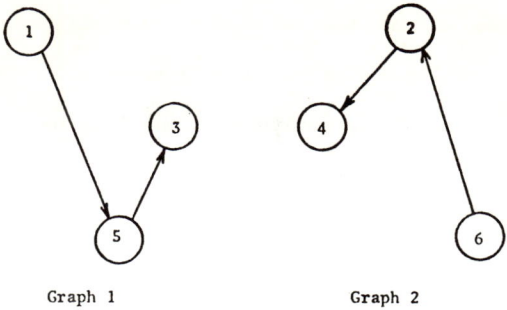

Figure 2.5 A Linear Graph Depicting Machine Orderings

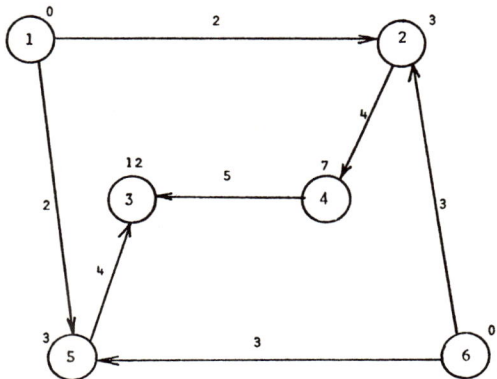

Figure 2.6 A Linear Graph Depicting Job Sequencings

chain. Following the above concept, the linear graph of Figure 2.6 consists of four types of L-level chains, where L = 0, 1, 2, 3. These chains are summarized below:

Zero-Level Chain	One-Level Chain	Two-Level Chain	Three-Level Chain
(1)	(1) << (2)	(1) << (5) << (3)	(1) << (2) << (4) << (3)
(2)	(1) << (5)	(1) << (2) << (4)	(6) << (2) << (4) << (3)
(3)	(2) << (4)	(2) << (4) << (3)	
(4)	(4) << (3)	(6) << (5) << (3)	
(5)	(5) << (3)	(6) << (2) << (4)	
(6)	(6) << (2)		
	(6) << (5)		

It is possible, however, to identify and count the number of L-level chains by constructing a set of non-quantified procedence matrices. A set of quantified precedence matrices can also be formed to find the lengths of the various paths having L-level chains.

<u>Non-quantified precedence matrix</u>. The above four L-level chains can be represented by the following non-quantified precedence matrices P^L, L = 0, 1, 2, 3.

$$P^0 = \begin{pmatrix} 1 & 0 & 0 & 0 & 0 & 0 \\ 0 & 1 & 0 & 0 & 0 & 0 \\ 0 & 0 & 1 & 0 & 0 & 0 \\ 0 & 0 & 0 & 1 & 0 & 0 \\ 0 & 0 & 0 & 0 & 1 & 0 \\ 0 & 0 & 0 & 0 & 0 & 1 \end{pmatrix}, \quad P^1 = \begin{pmatrix} 0 & 1 & 0 & 0 & 1 & 0 \\ 0 & 0 & 0 & 1 & 0 & 0 \\ 0 & 0 & 0 & 0 & 0 & 0 \\ 0 & 0 & 1 & 0 & 0 & 0 \\ 0 & 0 & 1 & 0 & 0 & 0 \\ 0 & 1 & 0 & 0 & 1 & 0 \end{pmatrix},$$

$$P^2 = \begin{pmatrix} 0 & 0 & 1 & 1 & 0 & 0 \\ 0 & 0 & 1 & 0 & 0 & 0 \\ 0 & 0 & 0 & 0 & 0 & 0 \\ 0 & 0 & 0 & 0 & 0 & 0 \\ 0 & 0 & 0 & 0 & 0 & 0 \\ 0 & 0 & 1 & 1 & 0 & 0 \end{pmatrix}, \quad P^3 = \begin{pmatrix} 0 & 0 & 1 & 0 & 0 & 0 \\ 0 & 0 & 0 & 0 & 0 & 0 \\ 0 & 0 & 0 & 0 & 0 & 0 \\ 0 & 0 & 0 & 0 & 0 & 0 \\ 0 & 0 & 0 & 0 & 0 & 0 \\ 0 & 0 & 1 & 0 & 0 & 0 \end{pmatrix}.$$

These L-level chain matrices are formed such that the nodes are assigned to successive rows and columns in ascending order. The elements in P^0 are such that

$$p^0_{k,\ell} = \begin{cases} 1, & \text{if } (k) = (\ell), \\ 0, & \text{otherwise,} \end{cases}$$

and those in P^1 are such that

$$p^1_{k,\ell} = \begin{cases} 1, & \text{if } (k) << (\ell), \\ 0, & \text{otherwise.} \end{cases}$$

Using the conventional matrix multiplication, we can identify the two- and three-level chains by computing the second and third power of the matrix P^1, respectively. The two- and three-level chain matrices P^2 and P^3 are shown above. In general, the elements in any L-level chain matrix can be computed such that

$$P^L_{k,\ell} = \sum_{r} P^{L-K}_{k,r} P^{K}_{r,\ell} ,$$

or in a matrix form

$$P^L = P^{L-k} P^K ,$$

where K is any non-negative integer such that $K \leq L$. It should be pointed out that P^L becomes a null matrix for integer $L \leq n$ which signifies the non-existence of any directed paths having chains of that level. It is obvious that in our case, P^4 is a null matrix because there are no four-level chains in the corresponding graph.

Each element in an L-level chain matrix $P^L_{k,\ell}$ represents the number of L-level chains. The total number of the directed paths having L-level chains can be obtained by summing all elements in the corresponding L-level chains matrix. As an illustration, the element $p^2_{1,3}$ whose value is one, indicates that there is one directed path containing two-level chains connecting node (1) with node (3). This path is (1) << (5) << (3). Also the sum of the elements in P^2 which is 5 is the number of paths having two-level chains. As a result, the total number of paths containing all numbers of direct-precedence relations (all chains) is simply determined such that

$$P = P^0 + P^1 + P^2 + \ldots + P^L$$

$$= (I - P^1)^{-1} ,$$

since P^1 is non-cyclic, and thus P^L must be zero for some power of L less than or equal to the number of nodes n. Each element in P represents the total number of paths connecting two nodes. For example, consider our case whose P is such that

$$P = P^0 + P^1 + P^2 + P^3 = \begin{pmatrix} 1 & 1 & 2 & 1 & 1 & 0 \\ 0 & 1 & 1 & 1 & 0 & 0 \\ 0 & 0 & 1 & 0 & 0 & 0 \\ 0 & 0 & 1 & 1 & 0 & 0 \\ 0 & 0 & 1 & 0 & 1 & 0 \\ 0 & 1 & 2 & 1 & 1 & 1 \end{pmatrix} .$$

The element $p_{1,3}$ whose value is 2 indicates that there are two different paths from node (1) to node (3), namely, (1) << (5) << (3) and (1) << (2) << (4) << (3).

Thus far, the main consideration has been given to simply identifying and counting the number of paths between nodes in a precedence matrix. This analysis can be extended, however, to include the lengths of the various paths. Note that the real value $t(k)$ attached to arc (k,ℓ) indicates the time to traverse this one-level chain.

Quantified precedence matrix. The lengths of the paths containing L-level chains can be represented in the quantified precedence matrices, Q^L, L = 0, 1, 2, 3.

$$Q^0 = \begin{pmatrix} \iota & 0 & 0 & 0 & 0 & 0 \\ 0 & \iota & 0 & 0 & 0 & 0 \\ 0 & 0 & \iota & 0 & 0 & 0 \\ 0 & 0 & 0 & \iota & 0 & 0 \\ 0 & 0 & 0 & 0 & \iota & 0 \\ 0 & 0 & 0 & 0 & 0 & \iota \end{pmatrix}, \quad Q^1 = \begin{pmatrix} 0 & 2 & 0 & 0 & 2 & 0 \\ 0 & 0 & 0 & 4 & 0 & 0 \\ 0 & 0 & 0 & 0 & 0 & 0 \\ 0 & 0 & 5 & 0 & 0 & 0 \\ 0 & 0 & 4 & 0 & 0 & 0 \\ 0 & 3 & 0 & 0 & 3 & 0 \end{pmatrix},$$

$$Q^2 = \begin{pmatrix} 0 & 0 & 6 & 6 & 0 & 0 \\ 0 & 0 & 9 & 0 & 0 & 0 \\ 0 & 0 & 0 & 0 & 0 & 0 \\ 0 & 0 & 0 & 0 & 0 & 0 \\ 0 & 0 & 0 & 0 & 0 & 0 \\ 0 & 0 & 7 & 7 & 0 & 0 \end{pmatrix}, \quad Q^3 = \begin{pmatrix} 0 & 0 & 11 & 0 & 0 & 0 \\ 0 & 0 & 0 & 0 & 0 & 0 \\ 0 & 0 & 0 & 0 & 0 & 0 \\ 0 & 0 & 0 & 0 & 0 & 0 \\ 0 & 0 & 0 & 0 & 0 & 0 \\ 0 & 0 & 12 & 0 & 0 & 0 \end{pmatrix}.$$

The elements in Q^0 which represents the times to traverse the paths of zero-level chains are such that

$$q^0_{k,\ell} = \begin{cases} \iota, & \text{if } (k) = (\ell), \\ 0, & \text{otherwise.} \end{cases}$$

Each node is assigned a zero magnitude value represented by ι (iota). This indicates that the time to traverse a zero-level chain is of a zero magnitude. The elements in Q^1 which represents the times to traverse the paths of one-level chains are such that

$$q^1_{k,\ell} = \begin{cases} t(k), & \text{if } (k) << (\ell), \\ 0, & \text{otherwise.} \end{cases}$$

As an illustration, the element $q^1_{4,3}$ whose value is 5 in the matrix Q^1 indicates that the time to traverse the one-level chain (4,3) is 5.

In general, the times to traverse paths of L-level chains are determined by computing the L-th power of the matrix Q^1 using a special matrix algebra. This algebra is equivalent, in terms of its postulates, to the conventional matrix algebra of non-negative matrices. The primary difference, however, is in its rules for additions and multiplications of matrices. To define the operations for addition and multiplication under this special matrix algebra, let a and b be nonnegative real values. Then,

1. the operation for addition of elements is performed such that
$$a * b = \max(a, b)$$
where $*$ is the symbol for the special matrix algebra addition;

2. the operation for multiplication of elements is performed such that
$$a \# b = \begin{cases} a + b, & \text{if } a, b > 0 \\ a, & \text{if } b = 1, a > 0 \\ b, & \text{if } a = 1, b > 0 \\ 1, & \text{if } a, b = 1 \\ 0, & a \text{ or } b = 0 \end{cases}$$
where $\#$ is the symbol for the special matrix algebra multiplication. Using the special matrix algebra, the lengths of the paths containing all L-level chains (chains of exactly L arcs) from node (k) to node (ℓ) are completed such that

$$q_{k,\ell}^{L} = *\sum_{n} q_{k,n}^{L-K} \# q_{n,\ell}^{K},$$

where K is any non-negative integer such that $K \leq L$. The symbol $*\sum$ is used to indicate a special matrix algebra summation. In a matrix form, the above relation becomes as follows:

$$Q^{L} = Q^{L-K} \# Q^{K}$$

The two- and three-level quantified precedence matrices, Q^2 and Q^3 are shown above. It is obvious that Q^L becomes a null matrix for some integer $L \leq n$, if any node (k) cannot be reached from any other node (ℓ) in any number of arcs (chains). In our case Q^4 is a null matrix.

Having formed the matrices Q^L, $L \geq 0$, we can define and compute the matrix Q whose elements represent the minimum time to traverse all chains connecting two nodes. This matrix is found such that

$$Q = Q^0 * Q^1 * Q^2 * \ldots * Q^L$$

As an illustration, consider our case whose Q is such that

$$Q = Q^0 * Q^1 * Q^2 * Q^3 = \begin{pmatrix} 1 & 2 & 11 & 6 & 2 & 0 \\ 0 & 1 & 9 & 4 & 0 & 0 \\ 0 & 0 & 1 & 0 & 0 & 0 \\ 0 & 0 & 5 & 1 & 0 & 0 \\ 0 & 0 & 4 & 0 & 1 & 0 \\ 0 & 3 & 12 & 7 & 3 & 1 \end{pmatrix}.$$

This indicates that, for example, the element $q_{2,3}$ whose value is 9 is the maximum length of time to traverse all chains of direct-precedence relations from node (2) to node (3).

It is of interest to continue the above development to find the earliest starting time of each operation (or node) in the graph of Figure 2.6.

<u>Earliest starting time vector</u>. In order to compute the earliest starting time of each operation, let us first define an initial starting time vector such that

$$S^0 = (s_k), \qquad k = 1, 2, \ldots, n,$$

where

$$s_k = \begin{cases} 1, & \text{if } (k) \text{ is unpreceded,} \\ 0, & \text{otherwise.} \end{cases}$$

The earliest starting time vector S can be computed such that

$$S = S^0 \# Q .$$

Considering our sample problem, the earliest starting time vector is

$$S = [1 \quad 3 \quad 12 \quad 7 \quad 3 \quad 1]$$

This indicates that nodes (1) and (6) can start at time zero, nodes (2) and (5) at 3, node (4) at 7, and node (3) at 12.

Another method to compute the earliest possible starting vector is to make use of the above relation as follows:

$$S = S^0 \# Q$$
$$= S^0 \# [I * Q * Q^2 * Q^3 * \ldots * Q^L]$$
$$= [S^0 \# I] * [S^0 \# Q] * [S^0 \# Q^2] * [S^0 \# Q^3] * \ldots * [S^0 \# Q^L]$$
$$= S^0 * [S^0 \# Q] * [(S^0 \# Q) \# Q] * [(S^0 \# Q^2) \# Q] * \ldots * [(S^0 \# Q^{L-1}) \# Q]$$
$$= S^0 * S^1 * [S^1 \# Q] * [S^2 \# Q] * \ldots * [S^{L-1} \# Q].$$

It is obvious that the last equation can be rewritten in a compact form such that

$$S = S^k,$$

where

$$S^k = S^{k-1} * [S^{k-1} \# Q^1], \qquad k = 1, 2, \ldots$$

The derivation of the above equation makes use of one of the properties of the special matrix algebra addition, namely, if Q is a matrix, then $Q * Q = Q$, for all Q. The earliest possible starting time vector can be obtained by successively computing the above equation until two successive vectors are identical. Applying this method, we get the same vector S after carrying out the computation four times. The reader is encouraged to carry out the above computation to find that vectors S^3 and S^4 are identical. The above method is referred to as the quasi-Boolean method.

2.3 Problem Assumptions

The shop scheduling problem as structured in the preceding sections is rather restricted from a practical point of view. It overlooks several important factors that are encountered in any operational system. For example, the flow of work in a shop production system is often interrupted by unpredictable events and hence, causes unexpected delays. These delays may be caused due to: (1) the probabilistic nature of machine breakdowns, (2) the variations in the performance of operators, (3) the absenteesim, (4) the delay in supplying materials, fixtures, or tools, (5) the changes that may be made in the specifications of jobs and the associated due-dates (6) the pressure of a customer for rushing his job which may delay some other jobs, (7) the rejection of some defective units which may cause either reworking operations for the defective units or splitting the job into two batches if the defective units cannot be reworked, and (8) the variability in processing times which depends on the methods of estimation.

Shop scheduling models that have been developed to date are based on a set of assumptions, the purpose of most of which is to simplify the analysis of the problem. These assumptions, however, increase the generality of the model. The assumptions include those placed on the characteristics of the jobs, machines, and processing times. These assumptions are:

1. Assumptions regarding jobs:

    1.1 Each job is processed according to a prespecified machine ordering, and no alternative ordering is permitted.

    1.2 Each job, once started, must be performed to completion, that is, no job cancellation occurs.

    1.3 Each job, once started on a machine, must be performed to completion before another job can start on that machine, that is, no preemptive priorities. In most cases this is a desirable feature.

    1.4 Each job is an entity, even though the job is composed of individual units. This eliminates job splitting between two or more machines. Assembly operations, in which units from different batches (jobs) are required, are also eliminated.

    1.5 Each job may not be processed by more than one machine at a time. This eliminates lap-phasing in which the same job is started on the succeeding operation as soon as some units are available from the preceding operation.

    1.6 Each job may have to wait between machines and hence, in-waiting inventory is permitted.

    1.7 Each job has a certain number of operations, each of which can be performed by only one machine.

1.8 Each job may have a due date, which is usually determined by the customer and shop management. Such a due-date, if any, is fixed.

1.9 Each job may be processed more than once on any machine.

2. Assumptions regarding machines:

2.1 Each machine center consists of only one machine, that is, there is only one machine of each type in the shop.

2.2 Each machine in the shop operates independently, and thus each machine is capable of operating at its own maximum rate of output.

2.3 Each machine is continuously available for assignment, during the scheduling period under consideration, without any interruption such as machine breakdowns or maintenance.

2.4 Each machine can process at most one job at a time. This eliminates the machines which are designed to process more than one job at a time such as multi-spindle drills.

3. Assumptions regarding processing times:

3.1 Processing times are known and finite.

3.2 Processing times may include implicitly job transportation times between machines, and machine setup and teardown times, if any. Transportation and changeover times may also be considered as negligible.

3.3 Processing times including changeover times, if any, are independent of the sequence in which the jobs are performed.

It should be pointed out that in the static problem case it is assumed that all jobs are known and ready to start processing before the scheduling period under consideration begins.

The above assumptions indicate how explicitly the conditions of a problem should be defined before a conceptual model can be used. As a consequence of relaxing one or more of these assumptions, different versions of the basic model have been analyzed. For example, Mitten [9], Johnson [8] and Nabeshima [11] have removed assumption 1.5 in an analysis of a two-machine flow-shop problem. The particular value of these studies is the possibility of introducing arbitrary start- and stop-lag which permit one to treat a variety of scheduling situations.

Furthermore, Heller and Logemann [7], among others, have removed assumption 1.9 in the development of an algorithm to generate and evaluate various schedules. This algorithm is based on certain properties of linear graphs. An operation of processing job j on machine m for the return i is referred to as a node (jmi). Of course, assumption 2.1 is dropped when we deal with identical machines in parallel or in hybrid, that is, in series and in parallel systems. In regard to assumption 3.1, various simulation experiments have been conducted to study the effect of uncertainty in processing times. Muth [10] has concluded that the schedule time is not very sensitive to moderately large errors in estimated processing times. Also Conway and Maxwell [2] have reported that errors of processing time estimates do not present a serious problem.

In the single-machine case where the changeover time is dependent on sequence, assumption 3.3 is normally invoked. For such a case, the changeover time must be separated from the processing time and there exists a unique changeover time for each pair of jobs. When the criterion is to minimize the total changeover time, it is of interest to mention that this class of problems is similar to the traveling salesman problem. The analogy is that a salesman must visit a number of cities once and only once and return to the city from which he starts. There is a unique distance between each pair of cities, and it is required to determine the sequence of cities that will minimize the total distance traveled. In terms of the above scheduling problem, each city corresponds to a job; the distance between cities corresponds to the changeover time for each pair of jobs; and the total travel distance corresponds to the total changeover time.

As would be expected, the abstract mathematical models that are amenable to analytical treatment are those which invoked the most simplifying assumptions. Considerable research has been done in attempting to develop efficient algorithms for arriving at optimal solutions. As in any operational systems the optimal solution is always relative to some measure of performance. The succeeding chapter will discuss these measures.

REFERENCES

[1] Ashour, S. and R. G. Parker, "A Precedence Graph Algorithm for the Shop Scheduling Problem," <u>Operational Research Quarterly</u>, Vol. 22, No. 2, 1971, pp. 165-175.

[2] Conway, R. W. and W. L. Maxwell, "Network Dispatching by the Shortest Operation Discipline," <u>Operations Research</u>, Vol. 10, No. 1, 1962, pp. 51-73.

[3] Cunningham-Green, R. A., "Describing Industrial Processes with Interference and Approximating their Steady-State Behaviour," <u>Operational Research Quarterly</u>, Vol. 13, No. 1, 1962, pp. 95-100.

[4] Elmaghraby, S. E., "The Machine Sequencing Problem - Review and Extensions," <u>Naval Research Logistics Quarterly</u>, Vol. 15, No. 2, 1968, pp. 205-232.

[5] Giffler, B., "Schedule Algebra: A Progress Report," <u>Naval Research Logistic Quarterly</u>, Vol. 15, No. 2, 1968, pp. 255-280.

[6] Heller, J., "Combinatorial Properties of Machine Shop Scheduling," Report NYO-2879, AEC Computed and Applied Mathematics Center, Institute of Mathematical Science, New York University, New York, N.Y., July 1959.

[7] Heller, J. and G. Logemann, "An Algorithm for the Construction and Evaluation of Feasible Schedules," <u>Management Science</u>, Vol. 8, No. 2, 1962, pp. 168-183.

[8] Johnson, S. M., "Discussion" Sequencing n Jobs on 2 Machines with Arbitrary Time Lags," <u>Management Science</u>, Vol. 5, No. 3, 1959, pp. 299-303.

[9] Mitten, L. G., "Sequencing n Jobs on Two Machines with Arbitrary Time Lags," <u>Management Science</u>, Vol. 5, No. 3, 1959, pp. 292-298.

[10] Muth, J. F., "The Effect of Uncertainty in Job Times on Optimal Schedules," Chapter 18 in <u>Industrial Scheduling</u>, (eds. J. F. Muth and G. L. Thompson), Prentice-Hall Inc., Englewood Cliffs, New Jersey, 1963.

[11] Nabeshima, I., "Sequencing of Two Machines with Start Lag and Stop Lag," <u>Journal of Operations Research Society of Japan</u>, Vol. 5, No. 3, 1963, pp. 97-101.

[12] Nugent, C. E., "On Sampling Approaches to the Solution of the n-by-m Static Sequencing Problem," Ph.D. Thesis, Cornell University, Ithaca, N.Y., 1964.

CHAPTER 3

MEASURES OF PERFORMANCE

The solution of the shop scheduling problem demands an explicit statement of a criterion or a set of criteria. A study of the criteria proposed in the literature indicates that a wide variety of measures of performance are employed. The variety of different scheduling situations and the prospects of obtaining solutions have usually influenced the choice of criteria. This chapter is devoted to discussing the characteristics of several types of criteria that have been proposed in the literature as well as those practiced in operational systems. In the process we shall define several basic terms, introduce the necessary notation, and discuss equivalences and interrelations among the various criteria.

3.1 Characteristics of Criteria

In a shop scheduling problem, the objective is to interrelate the work load, job due-dates, and the productive capacity such that the effectiveness of the shop is maximized and at the same time the customer's satisfaction is met. The effectiveness is measured in terms of various definable, quantifiable, and appropriate criteria (measures of performance). The terms "criterion" and "measure of performance" are used in this chapter interchangeably. The latter, however, places the emphasis on measurement and quantification. Some criteria correspond to certain desirable properties; whereas, others are associated with certain undesirable properties. Thus, while a particular alternate schedule may yield a good result with respect to a certain criterion, it may also lead to a poor result with respect to another criterion. It is therefore necessary to specify the relative importance of the various criteria involved and determine their interrelations.

In order to discuss a variety of criteria that have been proposed in the literature as well as those practiced in operational systems, we shall define several basic terms. Additional terms and concepts will be explained as they occur throughout the chapter.

Job release time. A job release time is the time at which a job is released to the shop after it has been engineered. It is equivalent to the earliest time that the processing of the first operation of a particular job could start. An alternative name is job ready time, or job arrival time.

Job completion time. A job completion time is the time at which the last operation of a particular job is completed. It is equivalent to the completion date of this particular job.

Job flow time. A job flow time is the length of time that a particular job spends in the shop. An alternative name is residence time, shop-time, or manufacturing interval. In the static case the job completion time is equivalent to the job flow time when the job release time is equal zero.

Job waiting time. A job waiting time is the length of time that a particular job has to wait before starting its next operation on a particular machine, in accordance with the prescribed machine ordering.

Job due-date. A job due-date is the time at which a particular job should be completed and delivered. It is equivalent to the time by which the processing of the last operation of a particular job should be completed. It can also be defined as the desired completion time.

Job allowable time. A job allowable time is the time allowed for a job to be in the shop. It can be interpreted as the difference between the due-date of a particular job and its release time.

Job lateness. A job lateness is the algebraic difference between the completion time and the due-date of a particular job, regardless of the sign of the difference.

Job tardiness. A job tardiness is the length of time that a particular job is completed after its due-date. Tardiness considers only the positive difference between the job completion time and its due-date.

Job earliness. A job earliness is the length of time that a particular job is completed ahead of its due-date. Earliness considers only the negative difference between the job completion time and its due date.

Machine idle time. A machine idle time is the length of time that a particular machine is not utilized before performing an operation.

Schedule time. A schedule time is the time interval between the release time of a set of jobs to the shop and their completion. It can be interpreted as a date of completion of a set of jobs, given that their release times equal zero. In such a case the schedule time can be defined as the maximum flow time of all jobs. An alternative name is maximum completion time, total elapsed time, makespan, or through put.

Shop utilization. A shop utilization is the ratio of the total work load to the available capacity of the machines in the shop in a given schedule period. The total work load may be expressed in terms of the total processing times to be scheduled on all machines. Similarly, the available capacity of machines may be expressed in terms of the time to be employed in performing the work. The shop utilization is, therefore, a fraction of the available machine capacity that is employed for performing the work load assigned. An alternative name is machine utilization.

Machine changeover. A machine changeover is the changing of the machine preparation to process a particular job after the preceding job has been completed. This may include both tearing down the jigs and fixtures used in processing the preceding job and setting up those which will be used in processing the succeeding job. An alternative name is machine setup.

In-waiting inventory. An in-waiting inventory is the jobs being worked on and waiting to be processed at a given machine. A job is in-waiting inventory at any time between the beginning and the end of its processing. An alternative name is work-in-process inventory.

Production rate. A production rate is the rate at which work flows through the operational system. The work may be measured in various units such as number, weight, volume, time, or value. An alternative name is output rate.

The measures of performance in a shop scheduling problem may take a number of different forms. Each of these measures is to be maximized or minimized to achieve the optimal usage of the machines to effectively perform the jobs. In trying to assess the "goodness" of a schedule, shop management might consider the following criteria: (1) Minimum machine changeover time or cost, (2) Minimum idle capacity including machines and manpower, (3) Maximum reserve capacity for rush orders, (4) Maximum shop utilization including machines and manpower, (5) Maximum production rate, (6) Minimum job handling in the shop, (7) Minimum in-waiting inventory,

(8) Minimum raw material and end-product inventory, (9) Meeting job due-dates, (10) Minimum schedule time, (11) Minimum late shipments, and (12) Minimum obsolescence and deterioration losses. This list clearly illustrates the multitude and variety of criteria that may affect the selection of a particular schedule. As Mellor [12] has pointed out, although, in real operational systems, most of these criteria are of great concern to management; no one has ever attempted to develop a scheduling model which combines them, operationally, to establish a total pay-off function.

As we attempt to classify the various criteria, some general characteristics considered to be significant, are encountered. For example, Conway [1] have emphasized the characteristics of jobs and the shop (or machines). <u>Job-attributed criteria</u> are characterized by their relation to jobs. The most obvious of these are the minimum job flow time criterion, the minimum job lateness criterion, and the minimum in-waiting inventory criterion. <u>Shop-attributed criteria</u>, on the other hand, are identified by their relations to the shop (or machines). Typical of such criteria is the maximum shop utilization criterion, the minimum machine setup time criterion, or the minimum machine obsolescence and deterioration losses criterion. However, when a criterion is a function of cost, it may be related to both jobs and the shop (or machines).

In his research, Gere [7] has distinguished the criteria as those which are based on the completion time of a set of jobs and those which are based on the due-date for each job. <u>Completion time-based criteria</u> are aimed at completing the jobs as soon as possible irrespective of the time at which any individual job is completed. Examples for such criteria include the minimum schedule time criterion, the minimum in-waiting inventory criterion, the minimum sum of completion time criterion, and the maximum shop utilization criterion. <u>Due-date-based criteria</u>, on the other hand, are aimed at optimizing the value of some function of the time at which individual jobs are completed, or optimizing the value of some parameter in cases where jobs are continually arriving at the shop. Typical of such criteria is the minimum number of late jobs criterion, the minimum total tardiness criterion, or the minimum cost of late jobs criterion.

Recently, Elmaghraby [6] has considered two types of criteria. <u>Job-related criteria</u> are those which distinguish between the jobs, and are therefore related to the position of each job in the sequence. Typical of such criteria is the minimum total tardiness criterion, the minimum total cost of production criterion, or the minimum in-waiting inventory criterion. <u>Sequence-related criteria</u>, on the other hand, are those which do not distinguish between individual jobs, but are related to a measure which is a function of the sequence. Typical of such criteria is the minimum schedule time criterion, or the minimum of maximum tardiness criterion.

The criteria, however, may be distinguished by one or more of the following characteristics:

1. <u>Time-based versus cost-based criteria</u>. Criteria can generally be described as either time to process or cost to process. Scheduling decisions may be completely affected by time-based criteria such as: (1) the minimum schedule time criterion--the time at which a set of jobs are completed; (2) the minimum flow time criterion--the length of time that a set of jobs spends in the shop; and (3) the minimum total lateness criterion--the difference between the completion times of particular jobs and their due-dates. On the other hand, scheduling decisions may be affected by cost-based criteria such as (1) the minimum cost of late delivery of jobs--the penalty cost associated with failure to complete the jobs by their due-dates; (2) the minimum cost of waiting jobs--the cost incurred due to the waiting of jobs before the machines; and (3) the minimum cost of idle machines--the cost incurred due to the idle time of the machines because of non-availability of jobs. The minimization of the total cost may be the most prevasive objective criterion in operational systems.

2. <u>Weight-based versus non-weight-based criteria</u>. In cases where a job has a priority over other jobs, it is usually given a weighted value which is a function of its relative importance. Similarly, in cases where certain expensive machines are involved, a set of weights that reflect the relative importance of these machines are usually determined to ensure their maximum utilization. Examples of such criteria include the minimum weighted sum of job completion times criterion, the minimum weighted sum of job tardinesses criterion, the maximum weighted machine utilization criterion. On the other hand, when all jobs are equally important as far as the

delivery date is concerned, or when all machines are equally important as far as utilization is concerned, the various criteria in which sequences are evaluated, are employed without any weight (or coefficient) associated with each job or machine. Typical of such criteria is the minimum schedule time criterion, or the maximum shop utilization criterion.

    3. <u>Single-based versus multiple-based criteria</u>. Single-based criteria require the evaluation of a single factor such as the minimum schedule time criterion, the minimum in-waiting inventory criterion, and the maximum shop utilization criterion. In practice, however, it is improbable that such criteria really reflect the ultimate objective of the shop. To achieve the overall objective of an operational system, it is necessary to optimize a multiple criterion which combines various single criteria. In such cases, scheduling decisions are always difficult to make because of the number of criteria involved and their often conflicting nature. While multiple criteria are of particular interest in practice, several single criteria are quite peculiar to the effectiveness of the shop. In the remainder of this chapter, our discussion of the various criteria, proposed and employed in practice, will follow the above classification.

3.2 Single Criteria

To give the reader more insight into the handling of single criteria and show some of the interrelations between them, we shall present a quantitative treatment of the following criteria:

1. Completion time criteria.
2. Flow time criteria.
3. Due-date criteria
4. In-waiting inventory criteria.
5. Utilization criteria.
6. Changeover criteria.

In the discussion which follows we shall use several notations, some of which will be required in later chapters. The basic notation used is:

    s_{jm_ℓ} starting time of job j on machine m_ℓ.

t_{jm_ℓ} processing time of job j on machine m_ℓ.

c_{jm_ℓ} completion time of job j on machine m_ℓ.

w_{jm_ℓ} waiting time of job j before being processed on machine m_ℓ.

$I_{j_k m}$ idle time of machine m before processing job j_k.

Additional notation will be defined as it occurs throughout the chapter. Our presentation will proceed in the following manner. We shall state the various forms of each criterion and follow, where it is appropriate, with significant remarks regarding interrelations and equivalences.

Completion time criteria

The most frequently used criteria that are simple, easy to measure, and related to other criteria are concerned with the completion time. Clearly, the completion time of any job is the sum of the time the job is released to the shop, the total processing time on all machines, and the total waiting time the job experiences while in the shop. Simply, the job completion time C_j is

(1) $$C_j = R_j + \sum_{\ell=1}^{M} t_{jm_\ell} + \sum_{\ell=1}^{M} w_{jm_\ell}$$

$$= R_j + T_j + W_j$$

where R_j, T_j, and W_j are the release time, total processing time, and total waiting time of job j, respectively. It is of interest to note that, in general, the release time and processing times of a job are known in advance. Therefore, the completion time of a job is dependent on the waiting time that job experiences in the shop.

The case of the single job can be extended to that of a set of J jobs. In such a case, the completion time of a set of J jobs corresponds to the maximum job completion time, referred to throughout this text as the schedule time and denoted by C^+. Hence, the schedule time associated with a sequence of J jobs can be stated as

(2) $$C^+ = \max_j [C_j] = \max_j [c_{jm_M}] = \max_j [s_{jm_M} + t_{jm_M}].$$

We shall encounter this criterion frequently in the succeeding chapters. It may be stated without proof that if the total waiting time of all jobs is a minimum, the corresponding sequence is optimal with respect to the schedule time. Note that in the dynamic case in which jobs arrive continually at the shop, the schedule time is not an appropriate measure.

In some theoretical studies as well as in practice, the means of certain measures and their interrelations are of interest. For a problem of J jobs, one can sum the completion times of all jobs, C_j, j=1,2,...,J, and then divide this sum by J to get the mean completion time such that

(3) $\bar{C} = \bar{R} + \bar{T} + \bar{W}$.

Again, as $\bar{R}$ and $\bar{T}$ are constants for a particular problem, the schedule which is optimal with respect to $\bar{C}$ is also optimal for $\bar{W}$. It can easily be verified that for any two sequences having the same schedule time (maximum completion time), the corresponding mean completion time may be different. For example, consider the (2x3) job-shop sample problem presented in Chapter 2. Two different sequences S' and S'' are represented by Gantt charts in Figure 3.1. The mean completion time of the sequence S' is

$$\bar{C}' = \frac{C'_1 + C'_2}{2} = \frac{14 + 19}{2} = 16.5,$$

and of the sequence S'' is

$$\bar{C}'' = \frac{C''_1 + C''_2}{2} = \frac{19 + 18}{2} = 18.5.$$

Although both sequences yield the same schedule time, $C^+(S') = C^+(S'') = 19$, the associated mean completion times differ.

It is intuitively obvious that for the single-machine case, the schedule time is sequence independent provided that the machine setup times are negligible or included in the processing times. In other words, the schedule time becomes constant regardless of the sequence of all jobs on the single machine. The sum of job completion times and mean completion time, however, are sequence dependent. This statement can easily be verified by considering two jobs 1 and 2 to be processed on a single machine. The corresponding processing times are 4 and 8, respectively. There are only two possible sequences. The sequence $S' = \{1\ 2\}$ yields a mean completion time of

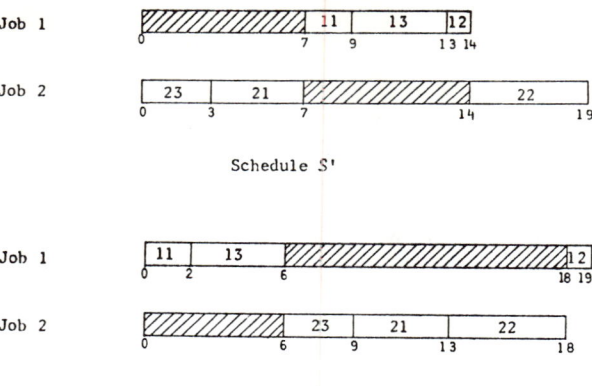

Figure 3.1 Job Flow Times of Schedules S' and S''

$$\bar{C}' = \frac{C_1' + C_2'}{2} = \frac{4 + 12}{2} = 8.$$

On the other hand, the sequence $S'' = \{2\ 1\}$ yields a mean completion time of

$$\bar{C}'' = \frac{C_1'' + C_2''}{2} = \frac{8 + 12}{2} = 10.$$

Furthermore, the sum of job completion times of S' and S'' are 16 and 20, respectively. Thus the sum of job completion times and mean completion time are sequence dependent. Note that the schedule time in both sequences is 12.

Flow time criteria

The job flow time criterion is one of the most important and intriguing notions in the study of shop systems. The flow time of a particular job is measured by the time that this job spends in the shop. Hence, by definition, the job flow time F_j can be expressed as

(4) $F_j = T_j + W_j.$

It can be seen from both equations (1) and (4) that the job flow time can be given as the difference between its completion time and release time, or simply

(5) $F_j = C_j - R_j$

Obviously, the mean flow time becomes

(6) $\bar{F} = \bar{T} + \bar{W} = \bar{C} - \bar{R}.$

One of the most interesting and important relations is that for a given schedule period, the mean flow time increases with the increase in the mean number of jobs in the shop. This relation will be verified later in this section, though it is intuitively obvious.

It should be pointed out that when the release time is zero, the flow time of that job becomes identical to its completion time and hence, the previous discussion regarding the completion time criteria is directly applicable to the flow time criteria.

Due-date criteria

The ability to meet preassigned job due-dates undoubtedly dominates other criteria. In practice, the due-date criteria are of the utmost importance because customers' reactions are frequently involved when delivery promises cannot be met. Basically, each job is assigned a due-date through negotiation between the customer and the shop management. In scheduling a set of jobs to meet their due-dates, the difference between the actual and promised completion times can be measured in three different ways: (1) lateness results when the actual job completion time does not coincide with the associated promised completion time; (2) tardiness focuses attention on jobs that are completed after their due-dates; and (3) earliness considers jobs that are completed ahead of their due-dates.

In some situations such as project systems, there are usually penalties to be paid to the customer for each day of delay in delivery beyond the contractual due-date. Management is very much aware of these penalty costs and usually strives to minimize or, if possible, eliminate these costs. In other situations such as shop systems, job lateness involves customer's reactions which are difficult to assess. Such reactions, however, will have serious implications in the long run. In general, as Gere [7] has pointed out, the penalty costs due to lateness include (1) executive time taken up in dealing directly with the customer through correspondence and telephone calls; (2) penalty clause in the contract, if any; (3) loss of good will resulting in an increased probability of losing the customer for some or all of his future orders; and (4) expediting because the jobs may have to be rushed through the shop at an extra setup cost and inefficient use of equipment and manpower. The complete elimination of job lateness must be brought at the expense of other factors such as increased in-waiting inventory and decreased shop utilization.

As mentioned earlier, the difference between the job due-date and its actual completion time can be measured in three different ways. First, when the completion time of a particular job fails to coincide with its respective due-date, the job is said to be late. Therefore, by definition, the job lateness L_j can be given by

(7) $\quad L_j = C_j - D_j$,

where D_j is the due-date of job j. Let A_j be the allowable time alloted a job j. Then, by definition, the allowable time of job j is expressed as

(8) $\quad A_j = D_j - R_j$.

Substituting equations (6) and (8) in equation (7), the job lateness can alternately be expressed in terms of job flow time,

(9) $\quad L_j = F_j - A_j$.

For problems consisting of J jobs, the mean lateness can be given by dividing the sum of job latenesses by the total number of jobs to yield

(10) $\quad \bar{L} = \bar{C} - \bar{D} = \bar{C} - \bar{A} - \bar{R} = \bar{F} - \bar{A}$.

Substituting equation (3) in equation (10) yields

(11) $\quad \bar{L} = \bar{T} + \bar{W} - \bar{A}$.

Since $\bar{R}$, $\bar{D}$, $\bar{A}$, and $\bar{T}$ are constants for a given problem, it follows from equations (10) and (11) that a sequence which is optimal with respect to $\bar{L}$ is also optimal for $\bar{C}$, $\bar{F}$, and $\bar{W}$.

Second, when the difference between the completion time of a job and its due-date is positive (that is, the job is completed after its preassigned due-date), the job is said to be tardy. Hence, by definition, the job tardiness T_j can be stated as

(12) $\quad T_j = \max [0, L_j]$.

It should be pointed out that the minimum total tardiness or minimum mean tardiness is often a more reasonable criterion than the minimum total lateness or minimum mean lateness, specifically, when it is important to get jobs done on time, or failing that, as soon as possible after their due-dates.

Finally, when the difference between the completion time of a job and its due-date is negative (that is, the job is completed prior to its preassigned due-date), the job is said to be early. Hence, by definition, the job earliness E_j can be expressed such that

(13) $\quad E_j = \max [0, -L_j]$,

In general, the job earliness is not an extremely useful criterion, since tardy jobs are usually the primary concern due to the obvious penalties they may invoke. In certain instances, however, although not resulting in an external form of cost arising from customer behavior, early jobs may give rise to an internal penalty resulting from their effects upon storage (end-product invenory) or even future planning.

The job lateness, tardiness, and earliness criteria are related to each other such that

(14) $\quad L_j = T_j - E_j$,

or in terms of means,

(15) $\quad \bar{L} = \bar{T} - \bar{E}$.

This relation holds true only in special cases such as: (1) if job due-dates are set so tight that all jobs are completed after their due-dates, then both lateness and tardiness are equivalent criteria; and (2) if job due-dates are set so loosely that all jobs are completed ahead of their due-dates or on time, then the earliness is simply the negative of lateness.

In-waiting inventory criteria

When more than one job exists in the shop, each job may compete at a certain time for a particular machine. This would result in an in-waiting inventory which consists of jobs forming a queue before each machine, waiting to be processed. The in-waiting inventory may be measured by one of the following: (1) total number of jobs in the shop N_s which consists of the number of jobs being processed N_p and the number of jobs waiting to be processed N_q; (2) total work content in the shop W_s which is the sum of the processing times for all jobs completed W_c, being processed

W_p, and remaining W_r; (3) work completed which is the sum of the processing times for all completed operations for all jobs in the shop W_c; or (4) work being processed and remaining which is the difference between total work content and work completed, or simply, $(W_s - W_c)$ or $(W_p + W_r)$.

Each of these measures may be appropriate under different situations. The number of jobs measure corresponds to situations in which there is a constraint on available space or in which the existence of the jobs in inventory encounters opportunity costs. Consider, for example, a car repair shop owned by one of the rent-a-car companies. The main objective in such a situation is to minimize the number of cars tied up in maintenance because these cars are not producing revenue. On the other hand, the work content measures correspond to situations in which funds tied up in inventory is important. For example, in a manufacturing system, one would be interested in expediting the jobs whose total work content or whose sum of work being processed and work remaining is highest. This is because such measures are considered equivalent to the investment in inventories which are both tying up funds and preventing or delaying revenue.

In considering the various measures of in-waiting inventory, it should be intuitively obvious that: (1) the mean number of jobs being processed $\bar{N}_p$ as well as the mean work being processed $\bar{W}_p$ becomes independent of sequence as the length of the schedule period increases; (2) the mean number of jobs waiting to be processed $\bar{N}_q$ determines the goodness of a sequence since it could ideally be eliminated completely; (3) the mean work remaining $\bar{W}_r$ would be an appropriate measure for the work backlog in the shop; and (4) the mean work completed $\bar{W}_c$ would be the best estimate of the in-waiting inventory cost. The effects of the in-waiting inventory measures in the shop have been investigated extensively by Conway [3].

In certain situations in which the number of jobs in the shop is considered as a measure of in-waiting inventory, it is of interest to verify the relation, stated earlier, that the mean number of jobs in the shop is directly proportional to the mean flow time for a given schedule period. Let us consider first the static case in which a finite number of jobs are simultaneously available in the shop. For convenience, let us assume that the release times of all jobs are $R_j = 0$, $j = 1, 2, \ldots, J$.

(Although the release times are taken to be zero for all jobs, its generalization can easily be considered by simply adding the value of the release time to all pertinent time denotations in the ensuing development.) Let us also assume that the jobs are numbered in the order of their completion, or simply, $0 \leq C_1 \leq C_2 \leq \ldots \leq C_j \leq \ldots \leq C_J = C^+$, where C^+ is the maximum completion time, and thus the schedule interval is $[0, C^+]$. As a direct consequence, job flow times become identical to job completion times and the schedule period becomes $[0, F^+]$, where F^+ is the maximum flow time.

The relationship between the number of jobs in the shop and job flow times is depicted in Figure 3.2. At time F_1, exactly $J-1$ jobs remain in the shop since one job has been completed. Continuing until time F_{J-1}, it is seen that a single job remains. Upon its completion, the shop becomes empty and the final time F_J is the maximum flow time F^+. The mean number of jobs in the shop $\bar{N}_s$ during the schedule interval $[0, F^+]$ can be computed from the ratio of the area under the graph of Figure 3.2 and the maximum flow time, or simply

(16) $\quad \bar{N}_s = \left(\sum_{j=1}^{J} (J-j+1)(F_j - F_{j-1}) \right) / F^+, \qquad F_0 = 0,$

$\quad\quad\quad = \left(\sum_{j=1}^{J} F_j \right) / F^+ .$

Dividing both numerator and denominator by J, we get

(17) $\quad \bar{N}_s = J\bar{F} / F^+ ,$

or equivalently,

(18) $\quad \bar{N}_s / J = \bar{F} / F^+$

This relation implies that for a given schedule period F^+ the mean in-waiting inventory, as measured by the number of jobs in the shop, is directly proportional to the mean flow time. The validity of the above relation is independent of the number of machines in the shop, the machine orderings of the jobs, the processing times of the operations, and the scheduling procedure employed.

The implication of the above relation can be extended further. It has been established in equation (6) that the mean flow time differs from the mean waiting time by a constant amount. As a consequence, for a given schedule period the mean number of jobs in the shop is directly proportional to the mean waiting time.

The above result can be proved under rather general conditions of job arrivals. Consider the dynamic case in which the jobs arrive intermittently during a certain schedule period with the interval $[\tau_1, \tau_2]$. Suppose that the shop process starts at time $\tau_1 = 0$ and ends at time $\tau_2 = C^+$, the maximum job completion time. Assume that J jobs are completed during that period. The jobs, numbered in the order of their arrivals, are released to the shop at times R_j such that, $0 \leq R_1 \leq R_2 \leq \ldots \leq R_j \leq \ldots \leq R_J \leq C^+$. Suppose that the jobs are completed at times C_j such that $0 \leq C_1 \leq C_2 \leq \ldots \leq C_j \leq \ldots \leq C_J = C^+$. This implies that the jobs are completed in their arrival order. (There is no loss of generality in having such an assumption, since the result holds equally true for any continuous process with arbitrary completion times.) Figures 3.3 shows the relation between the cumulative number of job arrivals and the cumulative number of job completions. Each horizontal section in the shaded area of the graph represents a particular job with flow time $C_j - R_j$, or simply F_j. Consequently, the mean number of jobs in the shop during the given schedule period $[0, C^+]$ is

(19) $\quad \bar{N}_s = \left(\frac{1}{C_J}\right) \sum_{j=1}^{J} (C_j - R_j) = \left(\frac{1}{R_J + F_J}\right) \sum_{j=1}^{J} F_j$.

Dividing both numerator and denominator of the right hand side by J, we get

(20) $\quad \bar{N}_s = \left(\frac{J}{R_J + F_J}\right) \bar{F}$,

or equivalently,

(21) $\quad \bar{F} = \bar{N}_s \left(\frac{R_J}{J} + \frac{F_J}{J}\right)$

As the number of jobs increases, the process becomes continuous, and as the steady-state is reached (provided that the arrival rate is less than the processing time rate), the term F_J/J tends to zero. Hence,

(22) $\quad \bar{N}_s = \left(\frac{J}{R_J}\right) \bar{F}$.

The term J/R_J, to be denoted by λ as in the context of queueing theory, represents the job arrival rate. Thus,

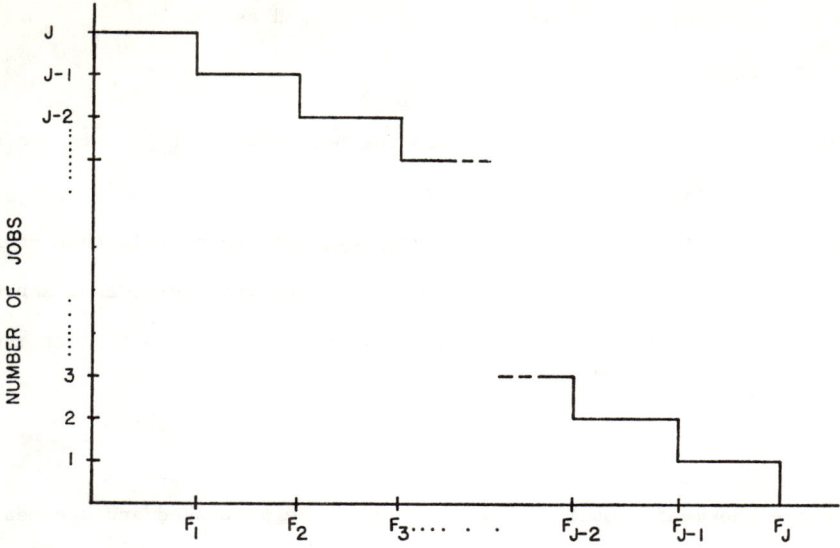

Figure 3.2 Number of Jobs Versus Job Flow Times

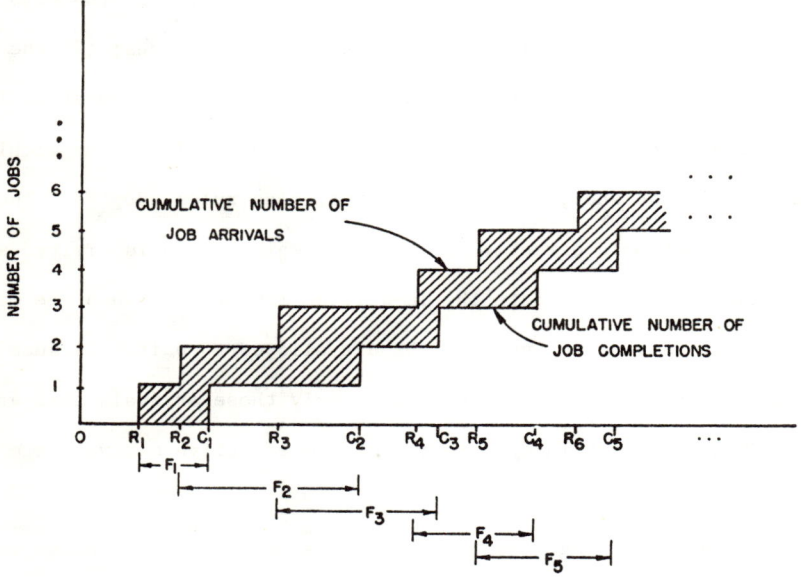

Figure 3.3 Cumulative Number of Job Arrivals Versus Cumulative Number of Job Completions

(23) $\bar{N}_s = \lambda \bar{F}$.

This relation has an immediate intuitive appeal if viewed as

(24) $\bar{F} = \left(\frac{1}{\lambda}\right) \bar{N}_s$,

which indicates that the mean flow time equals the mean number of jobs in the shop multiplied by the mean time between job arrivals.

We can deduce from this basic relation that any dispatching rule that minimizes the mean flow time must also minimize the mean in-waiting inventory, as measured by the number of jobs in the shop, providing that λ is constant. In a similar manner, it can be proved that

(25) $\bar{N}_q = \lambda \bar{W}$,

where $\bar{N}_q$ and $\bar{W}$ are the mean number of jobs waiting to be processed and the mean waiting time, respectively. Several proofs of the above relations are provided in [9,10,11].

The above results hold true for any shop under general stochastic conditions. The validity of both relations (23) and (25) is independent of: (1) the size of the shop, either in total number of machine groups or number of machines; (2) the pattern in which jobs are released to the shop as long as the shop is not saturated; (3) the characteristics of the processing times of the jobs in the shop; (4) the machine orderings of the jobs in the shop; and (5) the dispatching rules adopted. These relations, however, do not hold directly for shops in which there is limited storage space before each machine to accomodate the in-waiting inventory. When the maximum allowable storage space is reached, no new jobs are allowed to wait. In such cases, the job arrival rate λ can be redefined to include only those arrivals that are allowed to wait. When λ is redefined to represent the effective arrival rate $\hat{\lambda}$, the above relation can be made to hold.

In considering the in-waiting inventory cost as a criterion, the above measures hold true under very restrictive assumptions, namely, the in-waiting inventory cost is the same for all jobs and increases linearly with the waiting time of all jobs. This indicates that all jobs are considered to be of equal importance. This is not always the case in real life situations. In practice, however, it would be reasonable to expect that not only the values of the jobs in the shop are different, but also they increase as the jobs move through the shop. It will, therefore, be more realistic to take into account the actual value of each job at the time of waiting.

It is of interest to point out that for the single-machine problem, the minimization of the cost of carrying the job j in inventory until completed may be expressed as the minimization of the weighted sum of completion times, providing that the weights are the inventory costs incurred per unit time.

Utilization Criteria

The amount and nature of work to be performed in the shop and the increasing complexity of the shop itself cause the frequent occurrence of idle machines for various time periods. As a consequence, the productive capacity of the shop is said to be below full utilization. The idle time on a machine is dependent upon the completion time of a particular job on that machine and the availability of the succeeding job. The sum of idle times experienced by all machines, I can be given by

$$(26) \quad I = \sum_{m=1}^{M} \sum_{k=1}^{J} I_{j_k m} = \sum_{m=1}^{M} I_m,$$

where I_m is the total idle time on machine m. It may be stated without proof that if the total idle time on all machines is a minimum, the corresponding sequence is optimal with respect to the schedule time.

The machine idle time is an important measure for two reasons. First, it is very difficult to eliminate the idle time on all machines in a complex shop. Complete elimination of machine idle time creates large in-waiting inventory which may be more than the value that can be saved by eliminating machine idle time. Second, the machine idle time reflects the shop utilization and hence the loss of productive capacity due to lack of utilization.

Shop utilization is a very important economic consequence of scheduling decisions. The equipment in an operational system is usually a major capital expenditure, and as such is a fixed cost; depreciation has to be paid for it even if the equipment is not being used. It is obvious that efficient scheduling will allow a given work load to be performed in a short time, and thus maximize the utilization of the equipment. On the other hand, poor scheduling is costly, since it will always lead to the occurrence of idle machines which will be reflected in additional costs such as those of overtime and more shifts.

The shop utilization can be measured by the ratio of the work required to be processed in the shop to the available productive capacity employed in the shop in a given schedule period. In static problems, the schedule period is considered as the length of time starting with the earliest job release time and ending with the last job completion time. Since it is assumed in such problems that all jobs are simultaneously available, the schedule period becomes the maximum job flow time F^+. Hence the shop utilization U can be given such that

$$(27) \quad U = \left(\sum_{m=1}^{M} \sum_{j=1}^{J} t_{jm} \right) / F^+ = \left(\sum_{j=1}^{J} T_j \right) / F^+ .$$

Dividing equation (27) by M yields the mean shop utilization

$$(28) \quad \bar{U} = \left(\sum_{j=1}^{J} T_j \right) / MF^+ = [J\bar{T}] / MF^+ .$$

The above relation implies that the mean shop utilization is inversely proportional to the maximum flow time.

In dynamic problems, the mean shop utilization is a given parameter and not affected by the schedule. The mean shop utilization can be expressed in terms of the mean arrival rate λ such that

$$(29) \quad \bar{U} = [\bar{T}\lambda] / M,$$

where $\bar{T}$ is the mean amount of work per job (the mean job processing time on all machines). However, from equation (23), we have

$$(30) \quad \lambda = \bar{N}_s / \bar{F}.$$

Substituting for λ in equation (29), the mean shop utilization becomes

$$(31) \quad \bar{U} = [\bar{N}_s \bar{T}] / M\bar{F}.$$

This indicates that the mean flow time is inversely proportional to the mean shop utilization. Therefore, any dispatching rule that minimizes $\bar{F}$ also maximizes $\bar{U}$.

Utilizing the relationships between $\bar{U}, \bar{F}, \bar{C}, \bar{L},$ and $\bar{W}$ expressed in equation (6) and (10), the mean flow time can be expressed in several ways such that

(32) $\bar{F} = [\bar{N}_s \bar{T}] / M\bar{U} = \bar{W} + \bar{T} = \bar{C} - \bar{R} = \bar{L} + \bar{A}$

As mentioned earlier, the mean amount of work per job $\bar{T}$, the total number of machines in the shop M, the mean job release time $\bar{R}$, and the mean job allowable time $\bar{A}$ are constants. Hence, for any given problem with known values for $\bar{T}$, M, $\bar{R}$, $\bar{A}$, and $\bar{U}$, one can deduce very important relationship between the mean flow time $\bar{F}$, the mean number of jobs in the shop $\bar{N}_s$, the mean completion time $\bar{C}$, the mean waiting time $\bar{W}$, and the mean lateness $\bar{L}$. That is, any scheduling procedure which minimizes $\bar{F}$ also minimizes $\bar{W}$, $\bar{C}$, and $\bar{L}$.

Changeover Criteria

In certain situations, jobs may have similar setup requirements on machines and thus, changing from one job to another is simply a matter of changing tools or making necessary adjustments. For example, most of the jobs that need milling operation can be performed on milling machines with very little setup times that may be neglected or included in the processing times of the operations. Consequently, the machine changeover criteria become sequence independent. In other situations, however, it may be necessary to prepare each machine for performing a particular operation of a particular job and to teardown such a setup after this operation has been completed. For example, a gear cutting operation on the same milling machine requires mounting of special jigs and fixtures and setting them up according to the specification of the job. The setup time required to prepare the machine for the next operation depends on the operation that has just been completed on that machine. The time usually incurred in setting up and tearing down a machine is non-productive, and hence it reduces the potential machine capacity as well as the utilization of the entire shop. The machine changeover criteria becomes a sequence dependent and may be considered the dominant criteria for the evaluation of a sequence, especially if the variation of the setup requirements is considerably large with the change of sequence.

The changeover times incurred in changing the machine setup from processing a particular job to processing succeeding jobs on any machine, $t_{j_{k-1} j_k m}$ are placed in a setup time matrix. This matrix may be non-symmetric, since the time of the change from j_{k-1} to j_k may be different than the time of the change from j_k to j_{k-1}. The total changeover time for all machines H can then be expressed such that

$$(33) \quad H = \sum_{m=1}^{M} \left(\sum_{k=1}^{J} t_{j_{k-1} j_k m} + t_{j_J j_0 m} \right)$$

where

$t_{j_0 j_1 m}$ time required to change the initial setup of machine m to perform the first job in the sequence.

$t_{j_J j_0 m}$ time required to return machine m to its initial setup after the last job in the sequence has been completed.

In allowing a setup time for returning the machine to its initial setup after the last job in the sequence has been completed, the single-machine problem becomes analogous to the traveling salesman problem (this problem has been defined in Chapter 1). It is of interest to note that for single-machine problems in which the machine set up time depends on the sequence, the schedule time is minimized by selecting the sequence which has the minimum total set up time, since the total processing time is constant and thus it may be ignored. Furthermore, it is not difficult to see that a reduction in in-waiting inventory will necessarily lead to an increase in the total machine setup to satisfy the same work requires to be performed.

In certain circumstances such as those arising when some operations need special or intricate tooling is concerned, it may become more realistic to consider the number of setups, rather than the setup time. The total number of changeovers, G can be given by

$$(34) \quad G = \sum_{m=1}^{M} \left(\sum_{k=1}^{J} n_{j_{k-1} j_k m} + n_{j_J j_0 m} \right)$$

where

$n_{j_{k-1} j_k m} = \begin{cases} 1, & \text{if machine setup is required.} \\ 0, & \text{if machine setup is not required.} \end{cases}$

The term $n_{j_J j_0 m}$ may also be 0 or 1. The machine changeover measures (33) and (34) can be easily modified for the single-machine case by omitting the subscript m and the summation over m.

Sample Problem

We shall consider the (2x3) job-shop problem introduced in Chapter 2 as a sample problem to illustrate the various single criteria discussed thus far and to show the interrelations and equivalences between these criteria. The machine ordering and processing time matrices and job due-date vector are displayed below:

$$M = \begin{pmatrix} 11 & 13 & 12 \\ 23 & 21 & 22 \end{pmatrix}, \quad T = \begin{pmatrix} 2 & 4 & 1 \\ 3 & 4 & 5 \end{pmatrix}, \quad D = \begin{pmatrix} 12 \\ 16 \end{pmatrix}.$$

The machine changeover times are displayed in the following matrices in which each element represents the time required to setup machine m from performing job b if it is preceded by job a.

Machine 1

a \ b	0	1	2
0	-	5	2
1	5	-	3
2	3	4	-

Machine 2

a \ b	0	1	2
0	-	6	3
1	1	-	4
2	2	3	-

Machine 3

a \ b	0	1	2
0	-	6	3
1	4	-	2
2	5	4	-

Note that job 0 (dummy job) corresponds to the initial machine setup. For example, it requires 2 time units to set up machine 1 for performing job 2 first and 3 time units if that job is performed after job 1 on that machine. This sample problem is unrealistically small; however, because of its size, the problem can be handled easily such that all feasible sequences can be enumerated. This problem has 8 possible sequences, two of which are nonfeasible. The remaining six feasible sequences can be depicted by Gantt charts as shown in Figure 4.6 of Chapter 4. These Gantt charts are machine oriented. Job oriented Gantt charts can be depicted for all feasible sequences as those shown in Figure 3.1.

The evaluation of these feasible sequences with respect to the schedule time C^+, mean flow time $\bar{F}$, mean lateness $\bar{L}$, mean waiting time $\bar{W}$, mean idle time $\bar{I}$, mean shop utilization $\bar{U}$, mean number of jobs in the shop $\bar{N}_s$, and total machine changeover time H are displayed in Table 3.1. It is of interest to note that the optimal sequence S_4 with respect to $\bar{F}$ is also optimal for $\bar{L}, \bar{W}, \bar{I}$, and $\bar{U}$. This supports our equivalences' statements presented earlier in this section. Another interesting point emerges when the relationship between $\bar{F}$ and $\bar{N}_s$ is considered. Recall equation (18) which implies

Table 3.1 Sequence Evaluation of the (2x3) Job-Shop Sample Problem

Criterion	Feasible Sequences[+]					
	S_1	S_2	S_3	S_4	S_6	S_8
Schedule Time $C^+(S_i)$	14	13*	19	13*	19	18
Mean Flow Time $\bar{F}(S_i)$	13	12.5	16.5	10.5*	18.5	12.5
Mean Lateness $\bar{L}(S_i)$	-1	-1.5	2.5	-3.5*	4.5	-1.5
Mean Waiting Time $\bar{W}(S_i)$	3.5	3	7	1*	9	3
Mean Idle Time $\bar{I}(S_i)$	5.67	2.67*	7.33	2.67*	7.33	7.00
Mean Utilization $\bar{U}(S_i)$	0.452	0.487*	0.333	0.487*	0.333	0.352
Mean Number of Jobs in the shop $\bar{N}_s(S_i)$	1.86	1.92	1.74	1.61	1.95	1.39*
Total Machine Changeover Time $H(S_i)$	29*	29*	34	34	31	36

[+] Sequences S_5 and S_7 are non-feasible.

* Optimal sequence with respect to a particular criterion.

Table 3.2 Sequence Cost Evaluation of the (2x3) Job-Shop Sample Problem

Criterion	Feasible Sequences[+]					
	S_1	S_2	S_3	S_4	S_6	S_8
Job Waiting Cost $\beta(S_i)$	70	60	105	15*	150	30
Job Penalty Cost $\gamma(S_i)$	30	15	45	0*	115	10
Machine Idle Cost $\eta(S_i)$	112	60*	152	60*	144	136
Machine Changeover Cost $\delta(S_i)$	91	91	85*	85*	106	100

[+] Sequences S_5 and S_7 are non-feasible.

* Optimal sequences with respect to a particular criterion.

that $\bar{F}$ is directly proportional to $\bar{N}_s$ for a given maximum flow time F^+. Upon examining Table 3.1, it is apparent that among those sequences having similar values of F^+ (or equivalently, C^+ in this problem), the sequences which have minimum $\bar{F}$ also have minimum $\bar{N}_s$. For example, sequences S_2 and S_4 have identical C^+ or 13. The minimum $\bar{F}$ of 10.5 and the minimum $\bar{N}_s$ of 1.61 are associated with sequence S_4. Of course, it is also evident that such a relation between $\bar{F}$ and $\bar{N}_s$ cannot be founded for differing values of C^+. Furthermore, Table 3.1 shows that sequences S_1 and S_2 are optimal with respect to the total machine changeover time.

The various single criteria that have been discussed in this section have their own merits for being considered as measures of sequence evaluation. The succeeding section, however, deals with multiple criteria.

3.3 Multiple Criteria

In real situations, any one of the single criteria cannot be optimized at the expense of the others and thus, it is necessary and desirable to assess the alternate sequences with respect to a multiple criterion. However, it is different to assess the multiple criteria because of the fact that we are usually faced with a problem of attempting to achieve the best balance of the various single criteria, some of which may be conflicting. It would be no problem, however, if a schedule dominates all other alternate schedules with respect to all single criteria involved.

In selecting an alternate schedule, it may be necessary to minimize the schedule time as well as the flow time. These two measures are compatible; they decrease or increase together. On the other hand, it may be necessary to consider lateness and shop utilization as the pertinent measures for a given operational system. These two measures are diametrically opposed to each other in the sense that lateness is minimized if shop utilization is maximized. In other words, any substantial decrease in lateness would cause a concomitent increase in shop utilization.

To avoid the shortcomings of optimizing relative to a single criterion, it is necessary to consider simultaneously all pertinent criteria involved in an operational system. An appropriate pay-off function can be constructed using utility theory. The study of utility theory is beyond the scope of this text. However, it is worth mentioning three possible approaches, used in practice and provided by Elmaghraby [5], to resolve the problem of evaluating the alternate sequences with respect to multiple criteria. These approaches are: (1) composite evaluation approach, (2) sequential evaluation approach, and (3) constrained evaluation approach. We shall discuss the basic concepts of each approach and then follow with a sample problem for illustration.

Composite Evaluation Approach

The first approach, and perhaps the most evident of the three, involves the attachment of a weight to each single measure such that the combination of the various measures results in an overall or grand criterion. Effectively, the process of constructing an overall criterion is one of mapping each individual component of the generalized criterion onto a domain possessing a common scale of measurement. A frequently used measure of commonality is monetary cost.

The advantage of this approach is that less important or less influential single criteria can be treated as such by attaching respective weights to their desired impact upon the overall criteria. However, such a procedure meets with the same problem as that encountered with single measures when considered separately. That is, the problem arises as to what weight is to be associated with a given measure. If improper weights are attached to specific criteria, the net gain from the use of multiple criteria is essentially, neutralized and is possibly, even less beneficial than if single measures were used initially.

It is of interest to note that attachment of the contributive weights may be in some cases, not a problem of measurement, but one of judgment which ultimately gives rise to bias. This approach, however, is extensively used, especially when the weight of each measure is known.

Sequential Evaluation Approach

The second approach arises when particular single measures comprising the multiple criterion are ordered with reference to priority. The evaluative phase proceeds in such a manner that each measure is treated individually. Central to the scheme is the selection of the primary (most critical) criterion, ignoring for the time being all other criteria. Evaluation is carried out in such a manner that a feasible solution is obtained relative to the primary measure. If there is a unique solution, the procedure terminates. However, if there is more than one such solution that render the same evaluation of the primary criterion, a secondary criterion is evaluated among the alternate solutions obtained in the first phase. The procedure continues until either one optimal solution relative to a subset of measures results or all measures involved are exhausted.

One can consider this approach as a special case of the first approach. Optimization relative to a primary criterion is equivalent to optimization relative to the weighted sum of the criteria involved such that all criteria are assigned weights 0 except the primary criterion which is assigned the weight 1. The disadvantage of such an approach is that by its definition, slight variations in the evaluation of the primary measure tends to negate the effect of those criteria of lesser priority and could, possibly indicate a solution and subsequent decision that is inaccurate.

It is of interest to point out that this approach is used quite often, although not specifically mentioned. Most heuristic techniques for solving combinatorial problems, in general, and scheduling problems, in particular, employ certain tie-breaking rules. These rules are nothing more than secondary criteria and are used in precisely the capacity described above, namely to resolve ties resulting in alternate solutions based upon a certain primary criterion.

Constrained Evaluation Approach

The third approach is similar to the second in that it selects a particular criterion as the primary measure, but differs from it in its treatment of the other criteria. Essentially, the procedure is one of optimizing a primary criterion subject to the remaining measures as constraints upon the solution space. The use of such an approach is especially worthy in the case of diametrically opposed criteria. As stated earlier, two criteria are diametrically opposed to each other if the maximization of one tends to force minimization of the other. This approach is frequently used in situations where two measures only are involved. It is of interest to note that the structure of the primary criterion and the consequent constraints upon its evaluation, illicits the same type of difficulty as that encountered in the first approach in which weights were attached to each individual measure.

With the above discussions in mind, we proceed now with a sample problem to illustrate the three approaches that have been proposed.

Sample Problem

A sample problem should illuminate the application of the above three approaches. We shall consider the same sample problem that we have used in the preceding section. To render the results of the illustration below more meaningful and to give the reader some insight into the handling of cost measures, we consider first the evaluation of sequences with respect to the following cost criteria: (1) the minimum job waiting cost criterion, (2) the minimum job penalty cost criterion, (3) the minimum machine idle cost criterion, and (4) the minimum machine changeover cost criterion. We shall restrict ourselves to the opportunity costs of these criterion, since they reflect the opportunity loss as compared to an ideal schedule. An ideal schedule can be thought of as the schedule which does not cause machine idle times, job waiting times, or tardy jobs. Of course, such a schedule may not be feasible. However, the excess cost of an alternate schedule over the ideal schedule is the opportunity cost of this alternate.

These criteria can be measured as follows. First the opportunity cost due to job waiting β is given by

$$(35) \quad \beta = \sum_{j=1}^{J} \sum_{\ell=1}^{M} \beta_{jm_\ell} w_{jm_\ell}$$

where β_{jm_ℓ} is the cost per unit time job j waits to be processed on machine m_ℓ. Second, the penalty cost due to job tardiness γ is such that

$$(36) \quad \gamma = \sum_{j=1}^{J} \gamma_j T_j$$

where γ_j reflects the penalty cost per unit time job j is tardy. As defined earlier, T_j is the tardiness of job j. Third, the opportunity cost due to machine idleness η is given by

$$(37) \quad \eta = \sum_{m=1}^{M} \sum_{k=1}^{J} \eta_m I_{j_k m}$$

where η_m is the cost per unit time machine m is idle. Finally, the opportunity cost due to machine changeover δ is such that

$$(38) \quad \delta = \sum_{m=1}^{M} \left(\sum_{k=1}^{J} \delta_{j_k m} t_{j_{k-1} j_k m} + \delta_{j_0 m} t_{j_J j_0 m} \right)$$

where $\delta_{j_k m}$ is the cost per unit time incurred in changing the setup of machine m to perform job j_k after it has performed job j_{k-1}. The cost per unit time incurred in returning machine m to its initial setup after the last job j_J has been completed is denoted by $\delta_{j_0 m}$.

The evaluation of the feasible sequences of our sample problem with respect to the above cost criteria requires certain pre-determined values for $\beta_{j m_\ell}$, γ_j, η_m, and $\delta_{j_k m}$. Let the waiting costs per time unit be $10, and $5 for jobs 1 and 2, respectively, and the penalty costs $15 and $5 per unit time delay. Note that the actual values of each job at the time of waiting before the subsequent machines are considered the same. The costs incurred due to idle time are $4, 8, and 6 for machines 1, 2, and 3, respectively. The machine changeover costs are displayed in the following matrices in which each element represents the cost per time unit incurred in setting up machine m for performing job b if it preceded by job a.

Machine 1

a \ b	0	1	2
0	-	4	2
1	3	-	3
2	2	4	-

Machine 2

a \ b	0	1	2
0	-	2	5
1	4	-	3
2	2	5	-

Machine 3

a \ b	0	1	2
0	-	3	2
1	2	-	2
2	3	2	-

The interpretation of the above setup cost matrices is similar to that of the setup time matrices provided earlier.

The evaluation of the six feasible sequences with respect to the above cost criteria are shown in Table 3.2 (p. 56). It is of interest to observe that S_4 is optimal with respect to β and γ; whereas, sequences S_2 and S_4 are optimal with respect to η. Sequence S_3 and S_4 are optimal relative to δ. Now we illustrate the use of the three approaches for evaluating sequences with respect to multiple criteria. The reader should study each application critically, especially from the point of view of the relevance of other criteria and the effects of changing the criterion on the solution obtained.

1. <u>Composite evaluation approach</u>. Suppose that the total opportunity cost, as the multiple criterion, is composed of the four costs: (1) job waiting cost, (2) job penalty cost, (3) machine idle time cost, and (4) machine changeover cost. Since all costs reflect the same unit of measurement, the total opportunity cost, denoted by ψ, is the sum of the components of the above four costs, or simply,

$$\psi = \beta + \gamma + \eta + \delta .$$

The composite evaluation of each sequence S_i is displayed below

Criterion	S_1	S_2	S_3	S_4	S_6	S_8
Total Opportunity Cost $\psi(S_i)$	303	226	387	160*	515	276

This indicates that sequence S_4 is optimal with respect to the total opportunity cost as the composite criterion.

2. <u>Sequential evaluation approach</u>. With reference to our sample problem, assume that the four cost criteria are arranged in the following order in accordance with their importance: minimum machine idle cost, job penalty cost, minimum waiting cost, and minimum machine changeover cost. Optimization is first undertaken with respect to the minimum machine idle cost as the primary criterion. As shown in Table 3.2, the set of six alternate sequences is reduced to two sequences, namely S_2 and S_4. Consequently, optimization is then undertaken relative to the minimum job penalty cost as the secondary criterion. The results indicate that S_4 is a unique optimal solution. Such a decision can be shown below:

Criterion	S_1	S_2	S_3	S_4	S_6	S_8
Machine Idle Cost $\eta(S_i)$ (primary criterion)	112	60*	152	60*	144	136
Job Penalty Cost $\gamma(S_i)$ (secondary criterion)		15		0*		

Consequently, the procedure terminates such that S_4 is the optimal sequence relative to the minimum machine idle cost, as the primary criterion, and the minimum job penalty cost, as the secondary criterion. Had this secondary criterion not discriminated between S_2 and S_4, one would proceed in this manner until one runs out of either alternate optimal solutions or criteria, whichever comes first.

3. <u>Constrained evaluation approach</u>. Suppose that we wish to minimize the job penalty cost subject to the constraints upon the remaining cost criteria. Specifically,

consider the following optimization model:

Minimize

$$Z = \gamma(S_i)$$

subject to

$$\beta(S_i) \leq 50,$$

$$\eta(S_i) \leq 70,$$

$$\delta(S_i) \leq 95,$$

The solution of the above model can best be described as follows. For each constraint, the set of alternatives is reduced such that certain sequences are rendered non-feasible.

Constraint	S_1	S_2	S_3	S_4	S_6	S_8
Job Waiting Cost $\beta(S_i)$				15		30
Machine Idle Cost $\eta(S_i)$		60		60		
Machine Changeover Cost $\delta(S_i)$	91	91	85	85		

The resultant solution space, created by those sequences that satisfy the above constraints, indicates that only S_4 emerges. Consequently, the solution to the above model indicates that S_4 is optimal with reference to the job penalty cost and subject to the specific constraints upon the remaining criteria.

There are a number of variations which could be introduced into the model structure sited above. For example, various criteria may be unconstrained, hence, implying that their importance is negligible when compared to certain others.

Once the constituents (variables and parameters, assumptions and constraints, and measures of performance) of the shop scheduling model are identified and stated explicitly, the next step in the attainment of a solution is to find a suitable method of analysis. Various approaches for solving the shop scheduling problem can be found in the literature. The succeeding two chapters are devoted to the study of the combinatorial and statistical characteristics of the problem. It should be pointed out, however, that the basic objective in discussing these aspects is not so much to offer a method of solution as to examine several insights that they can provide.

REFERENCES

[1] Conway, R. W., "An Experimental Investigation of Priority Assignment in a Job Shop," Memorandum RM-3789-PR, Rand Corporation, Santa Monica, California, 1964.

[2] Conway, R. W., "Priority Dispatching and Job Lateness in a Job Shop," Journal of Industrial Engineering, Vol. 16, No. 4, 1965, pp. 228-237.

[3] Conway, R. W., "Priority Dispatching and Work-in-Process," Journal of Industrial Engineering, Vol. 16, No. 2, 1965, pp. 123-130.

[4] Conway, R. W., W. L. Maxwell and J. W. Oldziey, "Sequencing Against Due-Dates," Technical Report No. 6, Department of Industrial Engineering and Operations Research, Cornell University, Ithaca, New York, 1966.

[5] Elmaghraby, S. E., "The Role of Modeling in IE Design," Journal of Industrial Engineering, Vol. 14, No. 6, 1968, pp. 292-305.

[6] Elmaghraby, S. E., "The Machine Sequencing Problem-Review and Extensions," Naval Research Logistics Quarterly, Vol. 15, No. 2, 1968, pp. 205-232.

[7] Gere, W. S., Jr., "A Heuristic Approach to Job Shop Scheduling," Ph.D. Thesis, Carnegie Institute of Technology, Pittsburgh, Pennsylvania, 1962.

[8] Gupta, J. N., "Economic Aspects of Scheduling Theory," Ph.D. Thesis, Texas Tech. University, Lubbock, Texas, 1969.

[9] Jewell, W. S., "A Simple Proof of: $L = \lambda W$," Operations Research, Vol. 15, No. 6, 1967, pp. 1109-1116.

[10] Little, J. D., "A Proof of the Formula $L = \lambda W$," Operations Research, Vol. 9, No. 3, 1961, pp. 383-387.

[11] Maxwell, W. L., "On the Generality of the Equation $L = \lambda W$," Operations Research, Vol. 18, No. 1, 1970, pp. 172-174.

[12] Mellor, P., "A Review of Job Shop Scheduling," Operational Research Quarterly, Vol. 17, No. 2, 1966, pp. 161-171.

CHAPTER 4

COMBINATORIAL ASPECTS

The sequencing of a set of jobs on a number of machines gives rise to a problem of a combinatorial nature on which a time phasing problem of the most difficult type is superimposed. Although we have touched on the theoretical complexity of shop scheduling problems, which resides merely in the combinatorial nature of alternatives, we have not explicitly recognized the discussion as such. This chapter is devoted to discussing the combinatorial characteristics of the problem. The discussion is based on both sequences and schedules. In our analysis, the schedule time is used as the measure of performance. This treatment is intended to provide the reader with a great deal of insight into the nature of the problem. It should be pointed out that no attempt will be made at solving the problem.

4.1 Characteristics of Sequences

The selection of a sequence of jobs to be processed on a number of machines such that a given criterion is optimized may be obtained by the complete enumeration and evaluation of all alternative sequences. However, an exhaustive enumeration would not be a practical procedure because of the excessive number of sequences which would most likely have to be considered. One can appreciate the magnitude and complexity of the problem by considering the fact that there are $(J!)^M$ sequences for a problem of J jobs and M machines, in which each job has one, and only one, operation on each machine.

To demonstrate the enormous number of sequences as well as to discourage attempts at exhaustive enumeration, it should be sufficient to note that the number of sequences in which six jobs could be processed on three machines is $(6!)^3$ or over 3.73×10^8. An exclusive enumeration and evaluation of these sequences, at a rate of a microsecond each, would require over 100 hours of computer time. Due to the combinatorial characteristics of the problem, the number of sequences increases astronomically with problem size. For instance, in the case of six jobs and five machines there are $(6!)^5$ or approximately 1.93×10^{14} sequences which would require more than 6 years of computer time at the above rate. As a result, a complete enumeration approach is impossible for problems of practical size, even though computational abilities are increasing concomitantly with the development of faster and more powerful computers.

It seems likely that the way out of this dilemma is not to enumerate all possible sequences, but rather to generate only a small set of sequences with desirable characteristics. It is, therefore, reasonable to first identify the various sets of sequences. We shall consider a sample problem to illustrate the types mentioned. Subsequently, we shall attempt to develop some bounds on the number of sequences in each set.

Types of Sequences

Sequences may be conveniently identified by those characteristics which are associated with the precedence relations of both job sequencings and machine orderings, and with the potential values of the measure of performance. The relationship of the various sets of sequences is shown in Figure 4.1.

Possible sequences. In determining the complete set of possible sequences involved in a shop scheduling problem, the permutations of jobs on each machine should be first considered. Each machine can select any one of these permutations

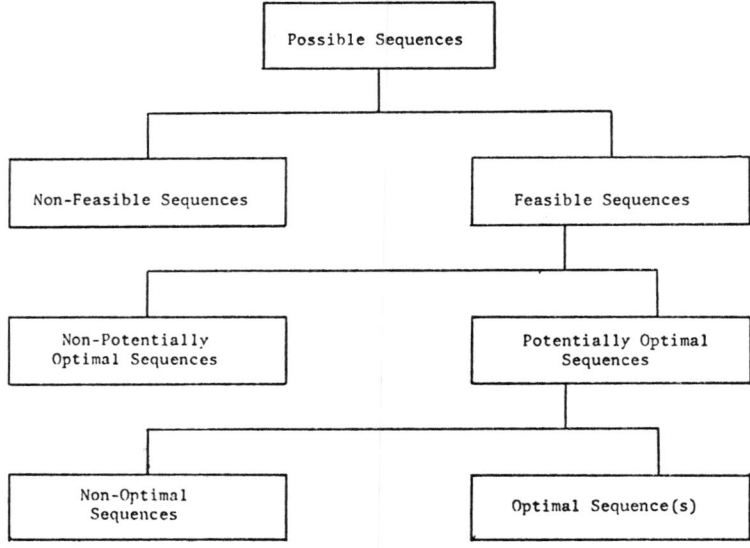

Figure 4.1 Types of Sequences

for processing. A possible sequence is, therefore, a combination of these permutations on all machines and may be represented by a job sequencing matrix. As defined in Chapter 2, a possible sequence is a collection of machine orderings and job sequencings.

Feasible sequences. Since the elements appearing in machine orderings are the same as those appearing in job sequencings, the precedence relations prescribed in the machine ordering matrix may be inconsistent with the precedence relations specified in the job sequencing matrix. As a result, a number of the possible sequences may not be technologically feasible. The non-feasible sequences must therefore be removed from consideration. The remaining set of sequences are feasible. A feasible sequence may be defined as a sequence in which the various operations must be performed according to the prescribed machine orderings. Specifically, a sequence is compatable or consistent with the machine orderings if the combined requirements do not permit an operation to precede itself.

To demonstrate the concept of consistency by using the precedence relations discussed in Chapter 2, consider a problem of two jobs to be processed on two machines. The technological requirements are represented by the machine ordering matrix M. Consider also a sequence in which the direct-precedence relations are represented by the job sequencing matrix, S_0. It is obvious that two types of constraints must be imposed: (1) machine interference constraints (that is, no more than one job can be performed on the same machine at the same time); and (2) precedence relation constraints (that is, no more than one machine can operate on the same job at the same time). The machine ordering matrix M and the job sequencing matrix S_0 are shown below:

$$M = \begin{pmatrix} 12 & 11 \\ 21 & 22 \end{pmatrix}, \quad S_0 = \begin{pmatrix} 11 & 21 \\ 22 & 12 \end{pmatrix}.$$

We wish to determine whether the sequence S_0 is feasible or not. First, from M, we have

1. $(12) \ll (11)$,
2. $(21) \ll (22)$.

This indicates that operation (12) directly-precedes operation (11); and operation (21) directly-precedes operation (22). Next, from S_0 we have

    3.   (11) << (21),

    4.   (22) << (12) .

It follows, however, from the direct-precedence relations 1 and 3 that

    5.   (12) < (21),

and from the direct-precedence relations 2 and 4 that

    6.   (21) < (12) .

Consequently, from the precedence relations 5 and 6, it follows that (12) must precede (12); and (21) must precede (21). This indicates that each operation precedes itself and hence, the sequence S_0 is inconsistent with the machine ordering matrix M.

    <u>Potentially optimal sequences</u>. There is a number of sequences which can never be optimal. Regardless of the values of processing times, such sequences, when evaluated, will have longer schedule times than certain other sequences. By logical elimination, the set of feasible sequences may be reduced to a set of potentially optimal sequences. These remaining sequences are said to dominate those sequences which belong to the set of non-potentially optimal sequences. A sequence from the dominated set has some undesirable job sequencings in which some operations are held up unnecessarily. In other words, a feasible sequence is non-potentially optimal, if one or more machines remain idle during a period of time sufficient to process one of the waiting jobs. It is possible, however, for non-potentially optimal sequences to yield a schedule time as good as a sequence from the potentially optimal set, but never better.

    <u>Optimal sequences</u>. Since the set of optimal sequences is a subset of the set of potentially optimal sequences, this dominant set is of great interest. It is, therefore, quite desirable if we can generate the set of potentially optimal sequences directly. However, it may be easier to search for the optimal solution from the set of feasible sequences rather than the set of potentially optimal sequences. The basic philosophy of various procedures employed in solving shop scheduling problems is directed towards conducting the search in a subset of the set of feasible sequences

that contains the optimal solution, or in devising schemes which can eliminate dominated sequences without complete enumeration and evaluation.

Elimination of Sequences

Having defined the various sets of sequences, it becomes appropriate to describe a number of procedures that can identify the non-feasible and non-potentially optimal sequences. It should be pointed out, however, that our objective in presenting these procedures is mainly to illustrate the various types of sequences.

Since the sequences which do not follow the specified machine ordering are technologically non-feasible, it would be desired to be able to eliminate the non-feasible sequences. Furthermore, since some of the remaining feasible sequences could not possibly be optimal, it would also be desirable to delete the non-potentially optimal sequences. The remaining potentially optimal sequences may then be evaluated with respect to a certain measure of performance to identify the set of optimal sequences.

The procedures, to be presented, employ various rules for identifying the non-feasible and non-potentially optimal sequences. We shall simultaneously present these procedures and work out a sample problem of two jobs and three machines. We have presented this sample problem in Section 2.2; however, for convenience, the corresponding machine ordering and processing time matrices are reproduced below:

$$M = \begin{pmatrix} 11 & 13 & 12 \\ 23 & 21 & 22 \end{pmatrix}, \quad T = \begin{pmatrix} 2 & 4 & 1 \\ 3 & 4 & 5 \end{pmatrix}.$$

The processing times are required only when the potentially optimal sequences are evaluated to find the set of optimal sequences.

Possible sequences. The elimination of non-feasible and non-potentially optimal sequences are systematically progressed by first constructing all possible sequences. For our sample problem, the number of possible sequences is $(2!)^3$ or 8. The job sequencing matrices associated with these sequences are displayed below:

$$S_1 = \begin{pmatrix} 21 & 11 \\ 22 & 12 \\ 23 & 13 \end{pmatrix}, \quad S_2 = \begin{pmatrix} 11 & 21 \\ 22 & 12 \\ 23 & 13 \end{pmatrix}, \quad S_3 = \begin{pmatrix} 21 & 11 \\ 12 & 22 \\ 23 & 13 \end{pmatrix}, \quad S_4 = \begin{pmatrix} 11 & 21 \\ 12 & 22 \\ 23 & 13 \end{pmatrix},$$

$$S_5 = \begin{pmatrix} 21 & 11 \\ 22 & 12 \\ 13 & 23 \end{pmatrix}, \quad S_6 = \begin{pmatrix} 11 & 21 \\ 22 & 12 \\ 13 & 23 \end{pmatrix}, \quad S_7 = \begin{pmatrix} 21 & 11 \\ 12 & 22 \\ 13 & 23 \end{pmatrix}, \quad S_8 = \begin{pmatrix} 11 & 21 \\ 12 & 22 \\ 13 & 23 \end{pmatrix}.$$

For example, the sequence S_1 indicates that job 2 precedes job 1 on all machines. The sequence S_5 implies that job 1 is processed before job 2 on machine 3; however, job 2 is followed by job 1 on machines 1 and 2. Note that a sequence indicates the sequencing of the two jobs on a particular machine; however, it provides nothing about the ordering of the machines for a particular job.

The above possible sequences may be displayed in a table. In constructing such a table, we consider the only two possibilities to sequence two jobs on each machine: either job 1 precedes job 2, or job 2 precedes job 1. These two possibilities can be given the following symbolic notation:

m job 1 precedes job 2 on machine m, that is, (1m) < (2m),

$\bar{m}$ job 2 precedes job 1 on machine m, that is, (2m) < (1m).

Using the above symbolic notation, we can enumerate the eight possible sequences in a table as follows:

Possible Sequences

	S_1	S_2	S_3	S_4	S_5	S_6	S_7	S_8
Machine 1	$\bar{1}$	1	$\bar{1}$	1	$\bar{1}$	1	$\bar{1}$	1
Machine 2	$\bar{2}$	$\bar{2}$	2	2	$\bar{2}$	$\bar{2}$	2	2
Machine 3	$\bar{3}$	$\bar{3}$	$\bar{3}$	$\bar{3}$	3	3	3	3

The above table can be constructed in a systematic manner by filling 2^{m-1} elements in row m, where m = 1, 2, 3, with barred and without barred machine indices alternatively starting with the barred ones. Each row represents a machine index. As an example, sequence S_5 merely implies that job 2 precedes job 1 on machines 1 and 2; while job 1 precedes job 2 on machine 3. It may be convenient to construct the above sequences in a binary notation form by replacing the barred machine indices with zero's and the non-barred indices with one's. The use of the binary notation simplifies the programming of this procedure on the computer.

Feasible sequences. The set of feasible sequences can be obtained by eliminating the non-feasible sequences from the set of possible sequences. Although inconsistency has been demonstrated earlier by a problem having only two jobs and two machines, Akers and Friedman [1] have extended the logic in a modifed form to the problem of J jobs and M machines. This procedure which employs Boolean algebra will be discussed using the symbolic notation.

In developing a rule for identifying the non-feasible sequences, let us consider the machine orderings for jobs 1 and 2 on a pair of machines, u and v, such that

1. $(1u) \ll (1v)$
2. $(2v) \ll (2u)$.

The above direct-precedence relations indicate that machine u directly-precedes machine v for job 1, but machine v directly-precedes machine u for job 2. Consider one of the possible sequences containing $\overline{uv}$ which implies the following direct-precedence relations on machines u and v:

3. $(2u) \ll (1u)$,
4. $(1v) \ll (2v)$.

The direct-precedence relations 1 and 4 imply

5. $(1u) < (2v)$.

The direct-precedence relations 5 and 2 imply

6. $(1u) < (2u)$,

which violates precedence relation 3. Thus, any sequence containing $\overline{uv}$ is non-feasible.

In general, if the machine ordering matrix of a problem having two jobs and M machines specifies that for each pair of machines u and v, where u must precede v for job 1 and v must precede u for job 2, then any sequence which specifies that job 2 precedes 1 on machine u and job 1 precedes job 2 on machine v, is non-feasible. Simply stated, any sequence which contains $\overline{uv}$ is non-feasible because each of the operations will be waiting for the completion of another and hence, none can be processed. The above principle leads to the following theorem [1]: A necessary and sufficient condition that a sequence of two jobs be feasible is that for each pair of machines, u and v, where u precedes v for job 1 and v precedes u for job 2, the term $\overline{uv}$ must not appear in the sequence. Accordingly, the rule for deleting the non-feasible sequence is summarized in Table 4.1.

Table 4.1 A Rule for Detecting Non-Feasible Sequences

Rule	Job	Partial Machine Orderings	Delete Sequence Containing
I	1	. . . u . . . v . . .	$\overline{u}v$
	2	. . . v . . . u . . .	

In our sample problem, the operations of job 1 must be processed on the three machines in the order (11) < (13) < (12). However, the operations of job 2 must be performed on these machines in the order (23) < (21) < (22). Applying the rule of Table 4.1 for detecting the non-feasible sequences, we first enumerate the machine pairs for each job. In this case, there are $\binom{3}{2}$ or 3 possible pairs. The precedence relations of the machine pairs are

Job 1:   1 < 3,   1 < 2,   3 < 2,

Job 2:   3 < 1,   1 < 2,   3 < 2.

Upon examining these precedence relations, it is apparent that the machine pairs 1 < 3 and 3 < 1 for jobs 1 and 2, respectively are in reverse order. Accordingly, the sequences which include the terms $\overline{1}3$ are non-feasible. Hence, sequences S_5 and S_7 are eliminated. The following feasible sequences are then retained:

Feasible Sequences

	S_1	S_2	S_3	S_4	S_6	S_8
Machine 1	$\overline{1}$	1	$\overline{1}$	1	1	1
Machine 2	$\overline{2}$	$\overline{2}$	2	2	$\overline{2}$	2
Machine 3	$\overline{3}$	$\overline{3}$	$\overline{3}$	$\overline{3}$	3	3

After the reduction of the complete set of possible sequences to a feasible set, there remains the task of extracting the potentially optimal sequences from the feasible set. However, before proceeding further to accomplish this task, we present two other procedures to test for consistency.

Since a non-feasible sequence is characterized by the existence of a loop among some of the operations, a given sequence may be examined for such a loop by a procedure developed by Marimont [15]. This procedure is based on setting out to expose any contradiction in a set of precedence relations. Such a contradiction would, of course, be the case when an operation precedes itself. The procedure employs Boolean matrices to represent the set of precedence relations.

As an illustration, we seek to test feasibility of the sequences S_1, S_5, and S_6. The directed linear graphs depicting the corresponding job sequencings are shown in Figure 4.2 to facilitate the construction of the precedence matrices. Each row or column expresses the precedence relations of the corresponding operation to the remaining ones. An entry of 1 in the matrix indicates that there exists a directed arc between the two nodes. An empty row or column implies that the corresponding operation is not dependent on any of the other operations. Note that if empty entries were filled with zeros, this matrix will be identical to that in Section 2.3. Operations with empty rows or empty columns are referred

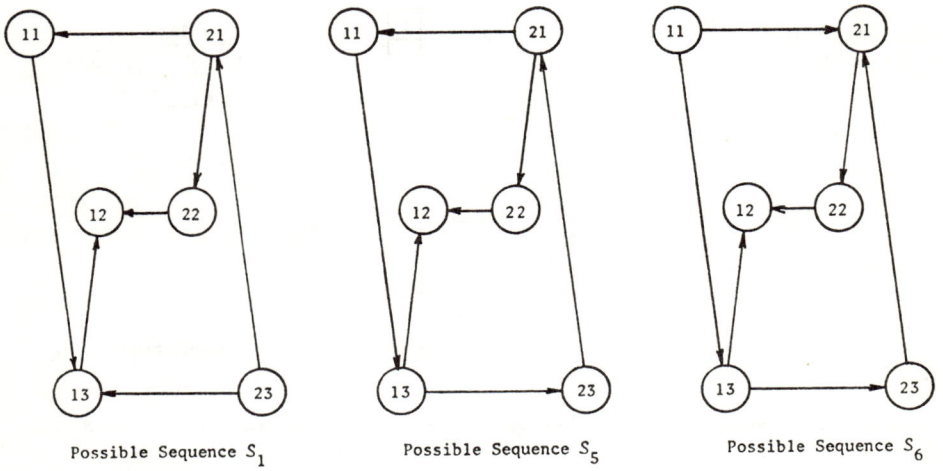

Figure 4.2 Linear Graphs Depicting Possible Sequences S_1, S_5, and S_6

to as schedulable operations (that is, these operations are available for scheduling) and hence, they are removed from the matrix. The reduced matrix is examined further in order to remove other operations which become available for scheduling. If all operations can be removed in this fashion, the reduced matrix will ultimately vanish implying that the sequence under test is feasible. In the case of a non-feasible sequence, the matrix cannot be reduced beyond a certain stage and the entries will show a loop among the remaining operations. Figure 4.3 shows that both precedence matrices of sequences S_1 and S_6 are vanished at the third stage and thus, S_1 and S_6 are feasible sequences. However, the precedence matrix corresponding to the sequence S_5 cannot be reduced beyond the third stage. Therefore, the sequence S_5 is non-feasible. In testing all possible sequences for consistency by this procedure, it appears that the sequences S_1, S_2, S_3, S_4, S_6, and S_8 are feasible.

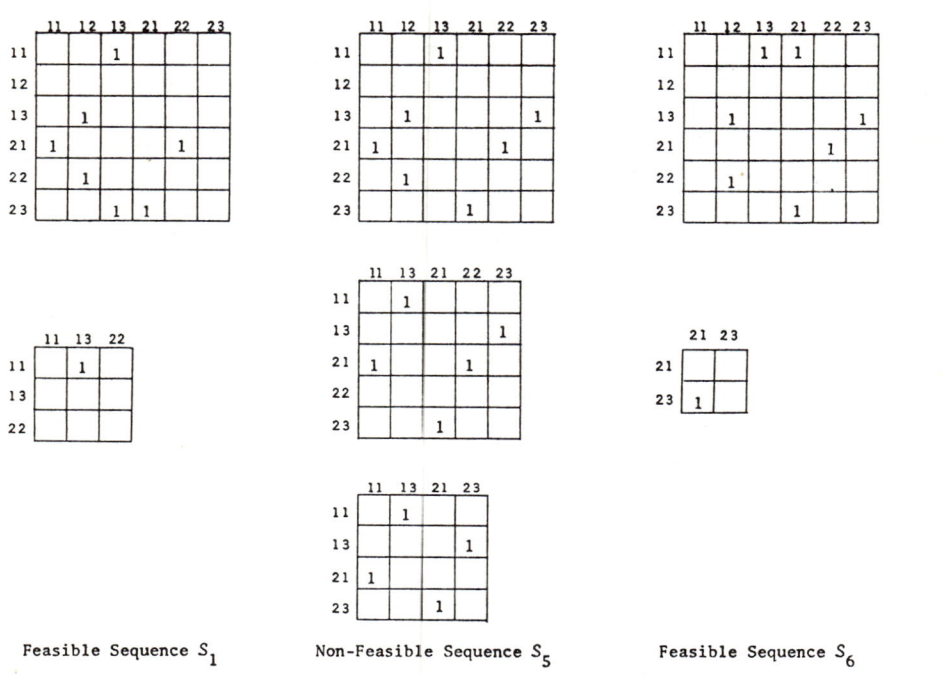

Figure 4.3 Boolean Matrices for Testing the Consistency of Sequences S_1, S_5, and S_6.

An alternative procedure of identifying a loop has been developed by Nelson [16]. This procedure involves studying the dependent relations among various operations. Figure 4.4 shows the trees of dependence which are prepared from the sequence S_1, S_5, and S_6. The numbers in the nodes represent operation indices and the small numbers beside the nodes represent the associated processing times. Note that the processing times are shown only for the nodes which comprise the longest branch in the dependent trees of sequences S_1 and S_6. These will be used in a later discussion. Essentially, we start with a node (0) and branch to any node or nodes according to the precedence relations in the corresponding linear graph. The first set of branches show the schedulable operations. Such a tree will terminate for a feasible sequence; whereas, it cannot terminate for a non-feasible because of the loop. Applying this procedure to all possible sequences, the results coincide with those obtained by the Boolean algebra and Boolean matrix procedures.

Potentially optimal sequences. The remaining feasible sequences may be examined to determine which sequence is potentially optimal. A feasible sequence may contain a machine on which the two jobs are processed consecutively in time and while this machine operates, all other machines are idle. Such a sequence is said to contain

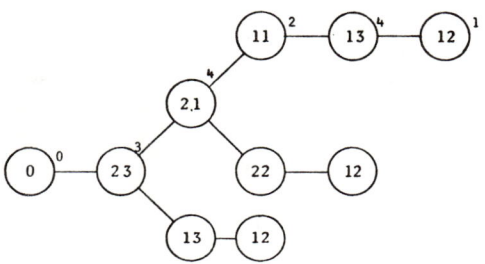

Feasible and Potentially Optimal Sequence S_1

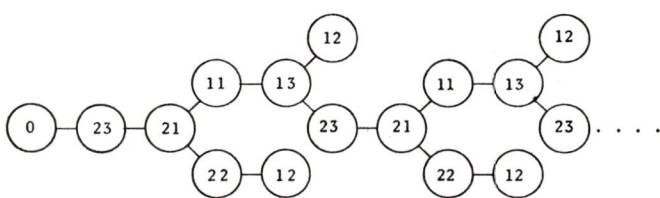

Non-Feasible Sequence S_5

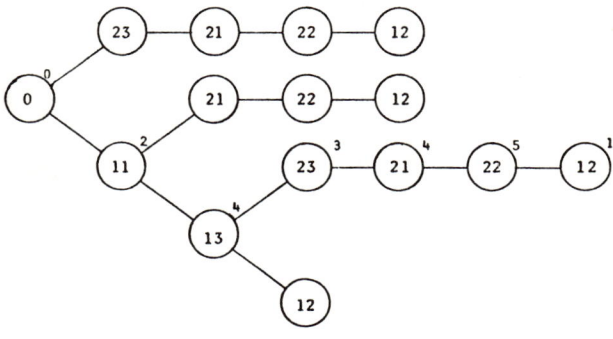

Feasible but Non-Potentially Optimal Sequence S_6

Figure 4.4 Dependent Trees for Testing the Consistency and Potential Optimality of Sequences S_1, S_5, and S_6

a free machine, and thus it is non-potentially optimal. The definition of a free machine indicates that all other machines remain idle for a period of time sufficient to process a job completely.

In general, the above characteristic leads to the following theorem [1]: A necessary and sufficient condition that a feasible sequence of two jobs belongs to the set of optimal sequences is that it contains no free machines. Elimination of sequences that contain free machines is carried out systematically by means of a set of rules summarized in Table 4.2 Note that rules I-III and V-VII are special cases of the basic rules IV and VIII, respectively.

Table 4.2 Rules for Detecting Non-Potentially Optimal Sequences

Rule	Job	Partial Machine Orderings	Free Machine	Delete Sequence Containing
I	1	v . . .	v	$\bar{v}$
	2	. . . v		
II	1	. . . u v . . .	v	$u\bar{v}$
	2	. . . u . . . v		
III	1	v . . . w . . .	v	$\bar{v}w$
	2	. . . u w . . .		
IV	1	. . . u v . . . w . . .	v	$u\bar{v}w$
	2	. . . u . . . u w . . .		
V	1	. . . v	v	v
	2	v . . .		
VI	1	. . . u . . . v	v	$\bar{u}v$
	2	. . . u v . . .		
VII	1	. . . v w . . .	v	$v\bar{w}$
	2	v . . . w . . .		
VIII	1	. . . u . . . v w . . .	v	$\bar{u}v\bar{w}$
	2	. . . u v . . . w . . .		

Applying the above rules to our sample problem, we observe that rules III and VII are applicable, since the last machine is the same for both jobs and the other two machines are in a reverse order. Consider machines v and w corresponding to machines 1 and 2, respectively in rule III of Table 4.2. This rule indicates that the sequence S_3 must be deleted because it contains the term $\bar{v}w$ or $\bar{1}2$. In applying rule VII, machine v and w correspond to machines 3 and 2, respectively. Thus, the sequence S_6 must be deleted, since it contains the term $v\bar{w}$ or $3\bar{2}$. As a result, the sequences S_3 and S_6 are non-potentially optimal. Thus, the following potentially optimal sequences:

Potentially Optimal Sequences

	S_1	S_2	S_4	S_8
Machine 1	$\bar{1}$	1	1	1
Machine 2	$\bar{2}$	$\bar{2}$	2	2
Machine 3	$\bar{3}$	$\bar{3}$	$\bar{3}$	3

are retained for further consideration. The definition of the free machine is best illustrated by plotting the Gantt chart of a sequence in which the horizontal bar represents a job rather than a machine. The sequences S_3 and S_6 are represented in this manner in Figure 3.1 as S' and S'', respectively.

The set of feasible sequences can be tested for detecting the non-potential optimal set by the dependent trees. This test depends on the fact that a tree is said to dominate another tree if all the branches of the former are contained in the branches of the latter. A dominated tree has some undesirable sequencings which hold up some operations unnecessarily. As can be shown in Figure 4.4, a tree can have several branches of varying lengths. The longest of these branches gives the schedule time for that sequence, since the length of a branch can be considered as the sum of the processing times of the operations along that branch. In certain instances, a tree might have a branch whose operations are contained in some other branch of the same tree. Such branches may be removed from the tree, since they cannot be the longest ones. Any of the remaining branches can become the longest one depending on the processing times.

In our sample problem, Figure 4.4 shows the dependent trees of the feasible sequences S_1 and S_6. The length of the longest branch in the dependent tree of sequence S_1 is

$$(0) \to (23) \to (21) \to (11) \to (13) \to (12)$$

with the total processing time of $(0 + 3 + 4 + 2 + 4 + 1)$ or 14. Similarly, the length of the longest branch in the dependent tree of sequence S_6 is

$$(0) \to (11) \to (13) \to (23) \to (21) \to (22) \to (12)$$

with the total processing time of $(0 + 2 + 4 + 3 + 4 + 5 + 1)$ or 19. The schedule times of sequences S_1 and S_6 are then 14 and 19, respectively. Hence, the dependent tree of sequence S_1 dominates that of sequence S_6. Examining the dependent trees of all feasible sequences, it appears that sequences S_3 and S_6 are non-potentially optimal, since they are dominated by the other sequences.

Optimal sequences. Having reduced the set of feasible sequences to a set of potentially optimal sequences, there remains the task of evaluating these sequences with respect to a certain criterion such as the schedule time, to find the optimal set. Given the processing time of each operation, the remaining sequences can be evaluated by plotting the corresponding Gantt charts. The following sequences:

Optimal Sequences

	S_2	S_4
Machine 1	1	1
Machine 2	$\bar{2}$	2
Machine 3	$\bar{3}$	3

are optimal with respect to the schedule time, since they are associated with the minimum completion time of 13.

To sum up, the various sets of sequences for our sample problem are as follows:

Possible Sequences: $S_1, S_2, S_3, S_4, S_5, S_6, S_7, S_8$

Feasible Sequences: $S_1, S_2, S_3, S_4, \quad S_6, \quad S_8$

Potentially Optimal Sequences: $S_1, S_2, \quad S_4, \qquad S_8$

Optimal Sequences (with respect to the schedule time): $\quad S_2 \quad S_4$

The determination of the number of sequences in the various sets poses an interesting problem which will be discussed in the succeeding subsection.

Analysis of Sequences

Thus far, our discussion has been concerned with defining and identifying the various types of sequences. In this subsection we shall attempt to develop some lower and upper bounds (or estimates) on the number of sequences in each set. These estimates, however, are merely of academic interest. We have emphasized earlier the fact that as soon as we attempt enumerating all possible sequences, we run into the combinatorial trap which generates a tremendous number of such sequences. Thus, the knowledge of the size of the various sets will certainly provide some idea of the amount of computational effort involved.

In considering the various sets of sequences, we first define some notation as follows:

N_1 number of possible sequences.

N_2 number of non-feasible sequences.

N_3 number of feasible sequences.

N_4 number of non-potentially optimal sequences.

N_5 number of potentially optimal sequences.

N_6 number of non-optimal sequences.

N_7 number of optimal sequences.

Referring to Figure 4.1 along with the above notation, the relations among the various sets of sequences are given such that

$$N_1 = N_2 + N_3$$
$$N_3 = N_4 + N_5$$
$$N_5 = N_6 + N_7 .$$

We shall then devote the remaining of this subsection to finding some expressions for the number of possible, feasible, and potentially optimal sequences, or N_1, N_3, and N_5, respectively.

Number of possible sequences. The number of possible sequences can be determined, for the case in which each job has one, and only one, operation on each machine, by considering the permutations of the jobs on each machine.

Specifically, J jobs can be arranged in J! possible ways on machine m, where m = 1, 2, ..., M. Each machine can select any one of these J! permutations for processing. As a result, there are $(J!)^M$ combinations of these permutations (or possible sequences).

On the other hand, if jobs have different numbers of operations and can return two or more times to a machine, the analysis of the combinatorics becomes very complex. Consider the case in which each of the J jobs has exactly K operations to be performed on a single machine. A lower bound on the number of possible sequences may be determined by presuming that all operations of each job are scheduled consecutively. Thus, the total number of possible sequences is $J^K(J-1)^K (J-2)^K \ldots 2^K 1^K$, or $(J!)^K$. Of course, this is the estimate of the number of possible sequences for the case in which each job has exactly one operation on each machine. An upper bound for such a case is $J^{J(K-1)} J!$. Hence, for a (Jx1) shop scheduling problem in which each job has exactly K operations, the lower and upper bounds on the number of sequences are

$$(J!)^K \leq N_1 \leq J^{J(K-1)} \quad .$$

Based on hand trials for small problems, the actual number of possible sequences is somewhat larger than the geometric mean of the upper and lower bounds. A reasonably good estimate of the number of possible sequences is $J^{K/2} (J!)^K$. To illustrate and compare the above estimates, Table 4.3 displays the different numbers of possible sequences for problems of various number of jobs and operations.

Table 4.3. Various Estimates of Number of Possible Sequences on a Single Machine

Number of Jobs	Number of Operations	Number of Possible Sequences			
		Upper Bound	Lower Bound	Approximate	Actual
J	K	$J^{J(K-1)}J!$	$(J!)^K$	$J^{K/2}(J!)^K$	
2	2	8	4	4	6
3	2	162	36	108	90
3	3	4,374	216	1,123	1,500
4	2	6,144	576	2,304	2,520
5	2	375,000	14,400	72,000	82,200

If each of the J jobs has a different number of operations K_j, where $j = 1, 2, \ldots, J$, the upper bound on the number of possible sequences becomes $(K_1 + K_2 + \ldots + K_j + \ldots + K_J)!$. In the general case where K_m, $m = 1, 2, \ldots, M$, represents the number of operations to be processed on each of the M machines, an upper bound is $(K_1!)(K_2!) \ldots (K_m!) \ldots (K_M!)$. As the number of machines increases, the upper bound becomes a very poor estimate.

While this much is known about the number of possible sequences, not much is known about the number of feasible or potentially optimal sequences. It should be pointed out that the estimates of the numbers of feasible and potentially-optimal sequences to be developed, are based on the cases in which each job has one, and only one, operation on each machine.

<u>Number of feasible sequences</u>. An expression for finding the number of feasible sequences of a (2xM) problem is presented by stating, without proof, the following theorem [1]: For a problem with 2 jobs and M machines, the number of feasible sequences, N_3 is expressed as the total number of r-tuples of machines with the same precedence relation, regardless of intervening machines, for both jobs, where $r = 0, 1, \ldots, M$. Or simply,

$$N_3 = 1 + M + \sum_{r=2}^{M} P_r ,$$

where P_r is the number of ordered r-tuples. An ordered r-tuple is defined as any set of r machines having the same precedence relations for both jobs.

As an illustration, consider our (2x3) sample problem used in the previous subsection. The number of feasible sequences N_3 is

$$N_3 = 1 + M + P_2 + P_3 = 1 + 3 + 2 + 0 = 6 .$$

Note that the value of P_2 is obtained by considering the precedence relations of the machine pairs which are

Job 1:   1 < 3,   1 < 2,   3 < 2,

Job 2:   3 < 1,   1 < 2,   3 < 2.

This indicates that the number of machine pairs having the same precedence relation P_2 is 2. It is obvious that there are no ordered triples and thus, P_3 is equal to zero.

In order to establish lower and upper bounds on the number of feasible sequences, let us consider the two extreme cases: (1) a flow-shop problem where all jobs have the same flow pattern (that is, each r-tuple has the same precedence relation for both jobs); and (2) a job-shop in which the flow patterns of both jobs are completely reversed (that is, every r-tuple appears in the reverse order). For example, consider the two extreme cases with the machine ordering matrices M_1 and M_2 shown below:

$$M_1 = \begin{pmatrix} 11 & 12 & 13 \\ 21 & 22 & 23 \end{pmatrix}, \qquad M_2 = \begin{pmatrix} 11 & 12 & 13 \\ 23 & 22 & 21 \end{pmatrix}.$$

The number of feasible sequences N_3 for the flow-shop problem with the machine ordering matrix M_1 is

$$N_3 = 1 + M + P_2 + P_3 = 1 + 3 + 3 + 1 = 8 \ .$$

Consequently, we conclude that all possible sequences for a flow-shop problem are feasible. This implies that for (2xM) problems, the upper bound on the number of feasible sequences is $(2!)^M$.

On the other hand, the number of feasible sequences N_3 for the job-shop problem having the machine ordering matrix M_2 is

$$N_3 = 1 + M + P_2 + P_3 = 1 + 3 = 4 \ .$$

It is obvious that a job-shop problem with any machine ordering configuration will have more than 4 feasible sequences, since some r-tuples may be in the same order. This indicates that the minimum number of feasible sequences (or the lower bound) is $1 + M$. As a consequence, for (2xM) shop scheduling problem, the bounds on the number of feasible sequences are

$$(1 + M) \leq N_3 \leq (2!)^M \ .$$

It should be quite clear that we can generalize the above result for (JxM) problems such that

$$(1 + M) \leq N_3 \leq (J!)^M \ ,$$

where the lower bound becomes a very poor estimate as the number of jobs increases. On the other hand, the upper bound is an exact estimate for flow-shop problems.

It may be of interest to consider the number of feasible sequences for a (Jx2) job-shop problem. The set of J jobs can be partitioned into four mutually exclusive subsets: (1) a subset $\{s_1\}$ includes n_1 jobs that require processing on machine 1 only; (2) a subset $\{s_2\}$ includes n_2 jobs that require processing on machine 2 only; (3) a subset $\{s_{12}\}$ includes n_{12} jobs that require processing on machine 1 first and then machine 2 second; and (4) a subset $\{s_{21}\}$ includes n_{21} jobs that require processing on machine 2 first and then machine 1 second. The total number of feasible sequences is

$$N_3 = (n_1!)(n_2!)(n_{12}!)^2(n_{21}!)^2 ,$$

since each subset can be considered as a flow-shop problem, and hence the associated possible sequences are feasible.

Number of potentially optimal sequences. Realistic estimates of the number of potentially optimal sequences is very difficult to obtain. One of the difficulties, as we shall presently see, stems from the fact that the types of measure of performance determine which feasible sequences are potentially optimal. We shall present some estimates of the number of potentially optimal sequences for flow-shop problems and special classes of job-shop problems.

For the (JxM) flow-shop problems, the set of potentially optimal sequences, contains only those sequences which have an identical job sequencing on the first two machines. This concept is based on theorem I which is as follows [7]: In scheduling a (JxM) flow-shop problem with respect to a regular measure of performance, one need consider only sequences in which the same job sequencing is prescribed on the first two machines. This would reduce the search for the optimal to $(J!)^{M-1}$ potentially optimal sequences. It follows that for (Jx2) flow-shop problems the number of potentially optimal sequences becomes $J!$ only. This implies that in searching for the optimal solution in two-machine flow-shop problems, it is sufficient to limit ourselves to the investigation of the set of permutation sequences. A permutation sequence is defined as the sequence which has identical job sequences on all machines.

For example, consider a (2x2) flow-shop problem having the following processing time matrix:

$$T = \begin{pmatrix} 4 & 9 \\ 3 & 2 \end{pmatrix}$$

A complete enumeration of the feasible sequences and associated schedule times and mean flow times appear below:

	$S_1^\dagger$	S_2	S_3	$S_4^\dagger$
Schedule Time	16	18	18	15*
Mean Flow Time	10.5*	13.5	17	14
Machine 1	$\bar{1}$	1	$\bar{1}$	1
Machine 2	$\bar{2}$	$\bar{2}$	2	2

Note that the starred value is an optimal solution with respect to an indicated measure of performance; and sequences marked † are those resulting from applying theorem I. It reveals from the above table that the set of potentially optimal sequences contains the permutation sequences S_1 and S_4. Obviously, S_1 is optimal with respect to the mean flow time and S_4 is optimal with respect to the schedule time. Thus, we conclude that in scheduling a (Jx2) flow-shop problem such that any regular measure of performance is optimized, the set of potentially optimal sequences contains only the permutation sequences, or simply

$$N_5 = j! \ .$$

By specializing the measure of performance, one can obtain a smaller set of potentially optimal sequences. For the (JxM) flow-shop problems, the set of potentially optimal sequences contains only those sequences that maintain the same job sequencing on the first two machines and the same job sequencing on the last two machines. This concept is based on theorem II which is as follows [7]: In scheduling a (JxM) flow-shop problem with respect to the schedule time, one need consider only sequences in which the same job sequencing is prescribed on the first two machines and the samy job sequencing is prescribed on the last two machines. This would reduce the search for the optimal to $(J!)^{M-2}$ potentially optimal sequences. It follows that for (Jx3) flow-shop problems, the number of potentially optimal sequences with respect to the schedule time is J!. This implies that it is sufficient in such a case to investigate only the set of permutation sequences, since they include the sequence which yields the minimum schedule time.

The following (2x3) flow-shop problem should illustrate the results of t
I and II. The following is the corresponding processing time matrix:

$$T = \begin{pmatrix} 5 & 1 & 1 \\ 1 & 5 & 5 \end{pmatrix}.$$

In a similar fashion, a complete enumeration of the feasible sequences and the corresponding schedule times and mean flow times are shown below:

	$S_1^{\dagger\#}$	S_2	S_3	$S_4^{\dagger}$	$S_5^{\dagger}$	S_6	S_7	$S_8^{\dagger\#}$
Schedule Time	12*	17	18	17	13	18	13	16
Mean Flow Time	11.5	16.5	17.5	16.5	10.5*	15.5	10.5*	11.5
Machine 1	$\bar{1}$	1	$\bar{1}$	1	$\bar{1}$	1	$\bar{1}$	1
Machine 2	$\bar{2}$	$\bar{2}$	2	2	$\bar{2}$	$\bar{2}$	2	2
Machine 3	$\bar{3}$	$\bar{3}$	$\bar{3}$	$\bar{3}$	3	3	3	3

Note that sequences marked † and ‡ are those resulting from applying theorems I and II, respectively. In applying theorem I, it appears that the number of potentially optimal sequences is $(2!)^2$ or 4. This set consists of the sequences S_1, S_4, S_5 and S_8. The sequence S_1 is optimal with respect to the schedule time. On the other hand, the application of theorem II, reveals that the set of potentially optimal sequences would contain the permutation sequences S_1 and S_8 only. The sequence S_1 is optimal since it yields a minimum schedule time of 12. Clearly, having had the mean flow time as the measure of performance, this set would not be potentially optimal, since it does not contain the corresponding optimal sequence. One can conclude that in scheduling a (Jx3) flow-shop problem such that the schedule time is minimized, the set of potentially optimal sequences consists of only the permutation sequences.

For flow-shop problems with more than three machines, however, a larger set of potentially optimal sequences should be considered to obtain the optimal with respect to any measure of performance. In other words, it is not sufficient to consider only the permutation sequences. For example, consider a (2x4) flow-shop problem with the following processing time matrix:

$$T = \begin{pmatrix} 5 & 1 & 1 & 5 \\ 1 & 5 & 5 & 1 \end{pmatrix}.$$

In a similar manner, a complete set of sequences along with the associated schedule times and mean flow times are displayed in the next page. Upon examining the table, it is apparant that the permutation sequences S_1 and S_{16} are not optimal. In fact, the sequence S_{13} in which job 2 precedes job 1 on machines 1 and 2, and job 1 precedes job 2 on machines 3 and 4, has the minimum schedule time and mean flow time.

Various upper bounds on the number of potentially optimal sequences for the (JxM) flow-shop problems can be developed. In extending the definition of a free machine for more than two jobs and applying a decision tree, a difference equation can be constructed. The solution of this difference equation provides the ratio of the number of potentially optimal sequences to the number of feasible sequences. Hence, an upper bound on the number of potentially optimal sequences can be found.

Next, we present two estimates on the number of potentially optimal sequences for special classes of job-shop problems. Consider first the (Jx2) job-shop problems that we have discussed earlier. This problem has been partitioned into four flow-shop subproblems: two single-machine and two two-machine subproblems. Thus, in considering only permutation sequences the number of potential sequences would be

$$N_5 = (n_1!)(n_2!)(n_{12}!)(n_{21}!) .$$

This estimate can be reduced by noting that the permutation sequences in both single machine subproblems do not affect any regular measure of performance and hence, the number of potentially optimal sequences becomes

$$N_5 = (n_{12}!)(n_{21}!) .$$

Finally, consider the extreme case of (2xM) job-shop problems in which the machine orderings of both jobs are completely reversed. Since this problem has been discussed earlier, it may be recalled that the number of feasible sequences of this problem is 1+M. In enumerating all feasible sequences, it is apparant that the sequence in which job 2 precedes job 1 on all machines and the sequence in which job 1 precedes job 2 on all machines (the first and last sequences in the table of possible sequences), contain free machines. These two sequences would never be optimal. Thus, for (2xM) job-shop problems the lower bound on the number of

	$S_1^{\dagger\ddagger}$	S_2	S_3	$S_4^\dagger$	$S_5^\dagger$	S_6	S_7	$S_8^\dagger$	$S_9^\dagger$	S_{10}	S_{11}	$S_{12}^\dagger$	$S_{13}^\dagger$	S_{14}	S_{15}	$S_{16}^{\dagger\ddagger}$
Schedule Time	17	22	23	22	19	24	23	22	18	23	24	23	14^*	19	18	17
Mean Flow Time	14.5	19.5	20.5	19.5	16.5	21.5	20.5	19.5	17.5	22.5	23.5	22.5	13.5^*	18.5	15.5	14.5
Machine 1	$\bar{1}$	1	$\bar{1}$	1	$\bar{1}$	1	$\bar{1}$	1	$\bar{1}$	1	$\bar{1}$	1	$\bar{1}$	1	$\bar{1}$	1
Machine 2	$\bar{2}$	$\bar{2}$	2	2	$\bar{2}$	$\bar{2}$	2	2	$\bar{2}$	$\bar{2}$	2	2	$\bar{2}$	$\bar{2}$	2	2
Machine 3	3	$\bar{3}$	$\bar{3}$	$\bar{3}$	3	3	3	3	$\bar{3}$	$\bar{3}$	$\bar{3}$	$\bar{3}$	3	3	3	3
Machine 4	$\bar{4}$	$\bar{4}$	$\bar{4}$	$\bar{4}$	$\bar{4}$	$\bar{4}$	$\bar{4}$	$\bar{4}$	4	4	4	4	4	4	4	4

potentially optimal sequences is

$$N_5 \geq M-1 \, ,$$

depending on the number of ordered r-tuples in each problem.

4.2 Characteristics of Schedules

Thus far, discussion has been concerned solely with the combinatorial characteristics of sequences. However, a frequent objective in the methods of analysis of shop scheduling problems is to determine the schedule, rather than the sequence, which optimizes a given measure of performance. It is, therefore, essential to digress and discuss the properties of schedules. Because of the insurmountable barrier which has been posed by the combinatorial nature of the problem, almost all methods of analysis are concerned with the generation of a reduced set of schedules which will always include a schedule(s) of a particular characteristics. It is quite natural that by a judicious choice of the schedules to be generated and by avoidance of undesirable schedules, great gains in computational tractability can be achieved.

This section will be devoted to the discussion of the combinatorial characteristics of schedules. Such a discussion will permit us to describe the various sets of schedules. We shall illustrate the types of schedules by the sample problem that we have been using in the preceding section. Finally, we shall attempt to devise some bounds on the schedule times and the distinct schedule times. As a reminder, the findings presented in this section are based on the minimum schedule time as a criterion.

Types of Schedules

The following observation is rather essential to the understanding of the types of schedules. We have shown in the previous section that a sequence specifies only the arrangements of a set of jobs on a number of machines. Regardless of processing times, the set of possible sequences must be tested for consistency to identify the feasible ones. These sequences do not provide the time at which each operation is performed nor the existence of idle times, if any, between operations. However, in associating the starting and completion times of operations with a specified feasible sequence, such a sequence becomes a schedule. A convenient way to present a schedule is by a Gantt chart. As we shall presently see, schedules are identified by those characteristics which are associated with quality (or goodness). The relationship of the various sets of schedules is displayed in Figure 4.5.

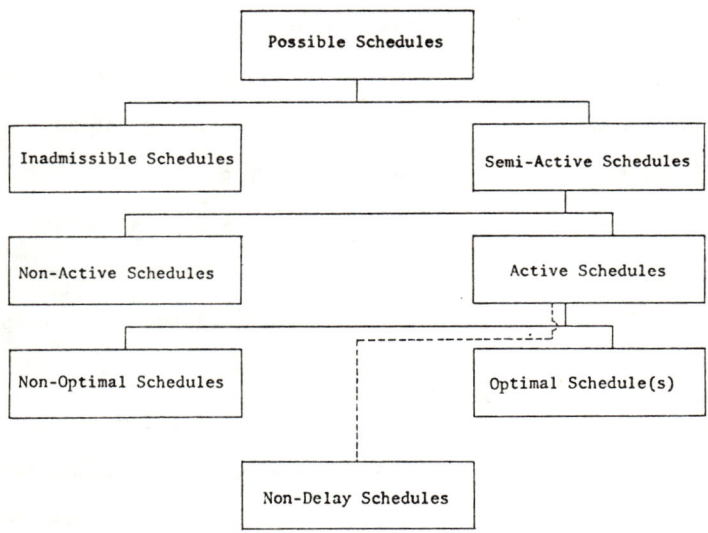

Figure 4.5 Types of Schedules

Possible schedules. A schedule, as defined in Chapter 2, is a feasible sequence in which the starting and completion times of the operations comprising all jobs on each of the machines are specified. As a consequence, the idle time between the processing times of each two successive operations, if any, can be specified. Regardless of the size of the problem, there exists an infinite number of possible schedules. This is because a different amount of idle times can be inserted between the operations in infinitely many possible ways. For example, consider the schedule S_1 shown in Figure 4.6. An amount of idle time can be inserted between operations (22) and (21) and the result is still a possible schedule. Thus, there exists an infinite number of possible schedules that possess identically the same sequence of jobs on each of the machines.

Semi-active schedules. Consider the infinite set of all possible schedules that can be produced from a particular feasible sequence. These schedules differ only in the amount of idle times which has been inserted between the various operations. A unique semi-active schedule can be found within this set of schedules. A characteristic of this semi-active schedule is that it dominates all other schedules in the set with respect to any regular measure of performance. The dominated set of schedules is said to be inadmissible set. In fact, any arbitrary inadmissible schedule can be converted into a semi-active schedule having the same sequence by the successive application of the limited-left-shift process. This is simply to shift each operation as far to the left as possible taking in consideration two aspects: (1) the sequence of jobs on each machine is maintained, and (2) the corresponding schedule, represented by a Gantt chart, allows no overlapping among operations.

When no operation can be shifted further by a limited-left-shift, the corresponding schedule is a semi-active one. For example, the six feasible sequences identified for the sample problem of the preceding section are evaluated and the associated semi-active schedules are displayed in Figure 4.6. An upper bound on the number of semi-active schedules for (JxM) problems in which each job has one, and only one, operation on each machine is $(J!)^M$. It should be obvious that this expression is exact for flow-shop problems, since all possible sequences are feasible.

Active schedules. Because of the enormous number of semi-active schedules, one can focus attention on a smaller set, referred to as the set of active schedules. An active schedule has the following properties: (1) no machine is idle for a period of time sufficient to perform a waiting job that could be completely processed; and (2) the processing of each operation starts as soon as the associated job and machine are available. Notice that a sequence which violates the first property, is non-potentially optimal sequence. The second property refers primarily to the schedule rather than the sequence. The essence of the set of active schedules is that it contains the optimal schedule(s).

A non-active schedule can become active by using the concept of left-shift. A left-shift process is simply a sequence of permissible interchanges of operations with

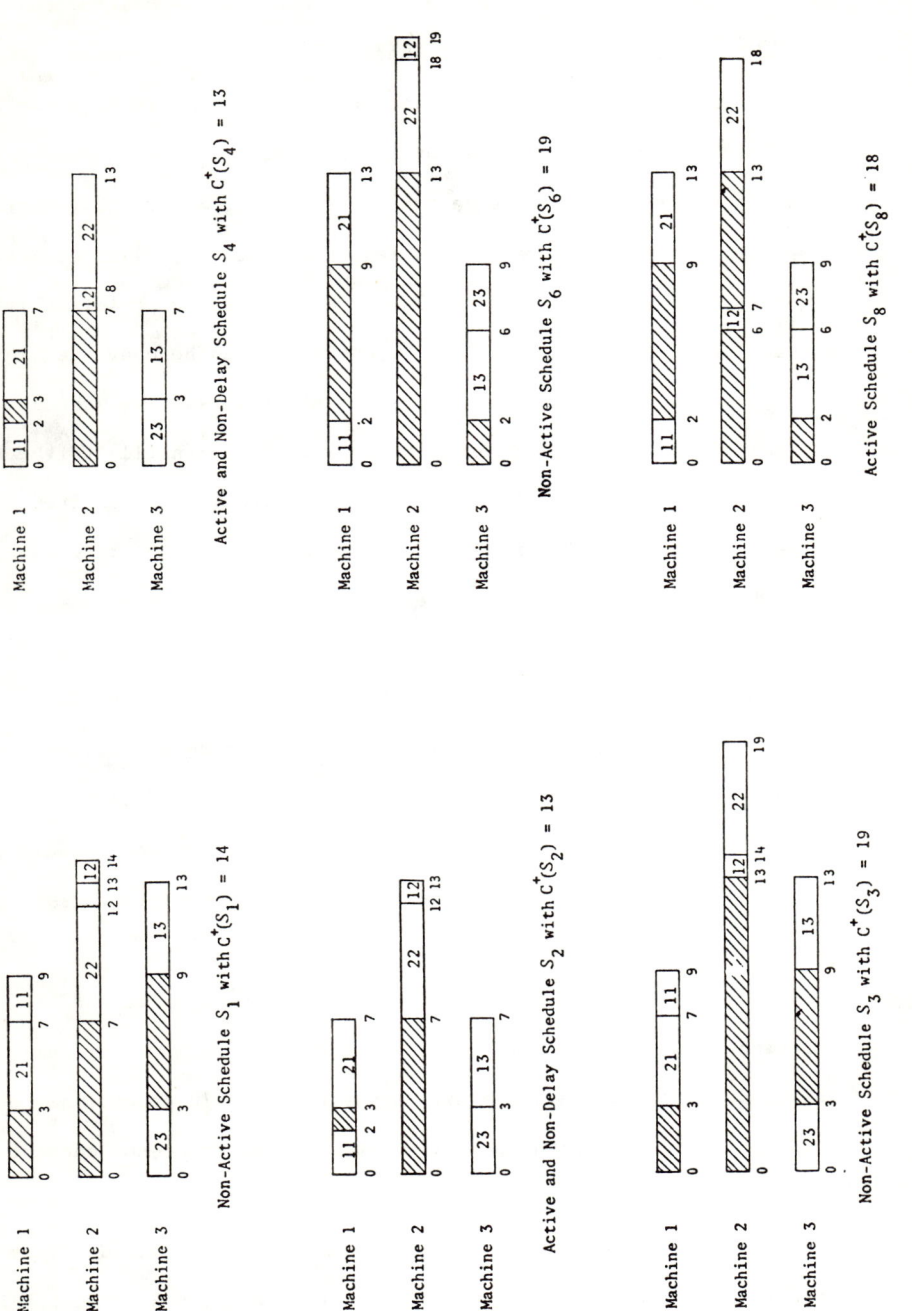

Figure 4.6 Gantt Charts Depicting Complete Set of Schedules of (2×3) Job-Shop Sample Problem

other operations or with idle times. Hence, active schedules may be defined as those in which a left-shift process is not possible. In applying the left-shift or the limited-left shift process, the machine orderings of jobs must be maintained. However, the limited-left-shift preserves the sequence of jobs on each machine (that is, it does not permit an operation to jump over another operation). Thus, a limited-left-shift is a left-shift but the converse is not true.

For illustration, consider the semi-active schedules S_1, S_2, S_3, S_4, S_6, and S_8 of Figure 4.6. No operation in any of these schedules is subject to a limited-left-shift. On the other hand, schedules S_2, S_4, and S_8 are active, since no left-shift is permissible. Non-active schedules S_1, S_3, and S_6, however, can be converted into active schedules S_2, S_4, and S_8, respectively. As an example, non-active schedule S_1 becomes active by using the left-shift process in moving operation (11) to the idle time interval [0, 2] on machine 1. Consequently, operation (12) is shifted to the left to occupy the interval [12, 13] on machine 2 and operation (13) to occupy the interval [3, 7]. Obviously, the result is the active schedule S_2.

An expression for the number of active schedules is likely to be very complicated. However, it has been reported that for a (6x5) job-shop problem in which the set of semi-active schedules is approximately eight million, there exist 84,802 active schedules [11]. A conservative estimate of the number of active schedules for a (6x6) job-shop problem is well over a million [8]. The number of active schedules, which increases very rapidly with problem size, depends on the values of processing times.

Non-delay Schedules. Due to the lack of success in finding an efficient procedure for enumerating the complete set of active schedules, one may rely on generating a set of non-delay schedules which may or may not contain an optimal schedule. The non-delay schedules are those active schedules which do not encounter any delay. Delay is defined as idle time incurred while a job is available for processing on the idle machine. For example, a detailed examination of the idle time intervals encountered in the active schedule S_8, reveals that machine 3 is kept idle during the time interval [0, 2], while job 2 has been available for processing since time zero. Hence, although schedule S_8 is active, it is not a non-delay schedule.

In our sample problem whose schedules are displayed in Figure 4.6, the active schedules S_2 and S_4 are non-delay schedules. By definition, the set of non-delay schedules is a subset of the active schedules.

Two brief remarks should be made. First, the set of non-delay schedules does not dominate the set of active schedules; whereas, the active schedules dominate the semi-active schedules. Second, an active schedule can be easily obtained from a semi-active schedule by using both left-shift and limited-left-shift processes; however, it is not so easy to construct a non-delay schedule from an active schedule.

In summary, the various sets of schedules for our sample problem are as follows:

Semi-active schedules:	S_1, S_2, S_3, S_4, S_6, S_8
Active schedules:	S_2, S_4, S_8
Non-delay schedules:	S_2, S_4
Optimal schedules (with respect to the schedule time):	S_2, S_4

The Gantt charts of these schedules are displayed in Figure 4.6. In order to fix the idea of the various types of schedules, we shall generate semi-active, active, and non-delay schedules.

Generation of Schedules

Our primary interest in this subsection is to show the procedure of generating a schedule with certain properties. We shall, therefore, not focus our attention on a particular method of solution to the shop scheduling problem. In an attempt to generate semi-active, active, and non-delay schedules, we shall make use of an algorithm based on certain properties of linear graphs. A linear graph representation of the scheduling problem has been presented in Chapter 2.

The various operations are arranged systematically in such a way that the set of schedulable operations can easily be identified at each stage. A schedulable operation is defined as an operation which is available to be scheduled and whose preceding operations have already been scheduled in accordance to the prescribed machine orderings. An operation is selected by a particular rule from the set of schedulable operations to be scheduled. Such a rule determines the type of schedule to be generated. The set of schedulable operations is then modified by replacing the operation just scheduled with its directly succeeding operation in accordance to the prescribed machine ordering. This procedure is repeated until the set of schedulable operations becomes empty which indicates that all operations are scheduled and the result is a schedule.

The generation of a schedule from each type is best illustrated with reference to the sample problem we have been using in the preceding section. For convenience, the corresponding machine ordering and processing time matrices are reproduced below:

$$M = \begin{pmatrix} 11 & 13 & 12 \\ 23 & 21 & 22 \end{pmatrix}, \qquad T = \begin{pmatrix} 2 & 4 & 1 \\ 3 & 4 & 5 \end{pmatrix}$$

The initial scheduling table is first constructed such that its columns designate the following:

- Q_1 operation designation
- Q_2 directly succeeding operation
- Q_3 index designates the state of an operation
- Q_4 processing time of an operation
- Q_5 index designates the sequence of a job on a particular machine
- Q_6 starting time of an operation
- Q_7 completion time of an operation

Each row in the table corresponds to one operation. The set of all operations are partitioned into as many groups as the number of machines and placed under Q_1. The directly succeeding operations to those under Q_1 are placed under Q_2. The processing times of the operations under Q_1 are listed under Q_4. Any operation can be in one, and only one, of three states: not available for scheduling, schedulable, or already scheduled. Consequently, the index which designates the state of the operation (jm) under Q_3 can be such that

1. $Q_3(jm) = 1$ which indicates that operation (jm) is not available for scheduling;

2. $Q_3(jm) = 0$ which indicates that operation (jm) is schedulable; or

3. $Q_3(jm) = -1$ which indicates that operation (jm) has been scheduled.

The initial scheduling table for our sample problem appears later in Table 4.4.

To illustrate the various types of schedules, we shall make use of the following algorithm [2]. This computational algorithm is general in the sense that any type of schedule can be generated depending on the scheduling rule utilized in step 2. The formal steps of the algorithm are as follows:

Step 1: Construct the initial scheduling table.

Step 2: Select one of the schedulable operations $(j_0 m_0)$ by a particular rule.

Step 3: Index the job sequence on the assigned machine by setting

$$k = \max_j \left(Q_5(jm_0) \right),$$

and check k such that

3.1 If $k = 0$, set $Q_5(j_0 m_0) = 1$ and go to step 5.

3.2 If $k \neq 0$, set $Q_5(j_0 m_0) = k + 1$ and go to step 4.

Step 4: Compute the starting time of the selected operation such that

$$Q_6(j_0 m_0) = \max \left(Q_6(j_0 m_0), Q_7(jm_0) \right),$$

given that $Q_5(jm_0) = k$.

Step 5: Compute the completion time of the selected operation such that

$$Q_7(j_0 m_0) = Q_6(j_0 m_0) + Q_4(j_0 m_0).$$

Step 6: Set the status index of the selected operation such that

$$Q_3(j_0 m_0) = -1$$

to indicate that this operation has been scheduled.

Step 7: Update the potential starting time of the directly succeeding operation such that

7.1 If there is an operation $(j_0 m)$ directly succeeding operation $(j_0 m_0)$, set

$$Q_6(j_0 m) = \max \left(Q_6(j_0 m), Q_7(j_0 m_0) \right),$$

and

$$Q_3(j_0 m) = 0,$$

and go to step 8.

7.2 If there is no such an operation, go to step 8.

Step 8: Check the set of schedulable operations such that

8.1 If one or more operations having

$$Q_3(jm) = 0 \text{ or } 1,$$

go to step 2.

8.2 If all operations having

$$Q_3(jm) = -1,$$

go to step 9.

Step 9: Find the schedule time of the resulting schedule such that

$$C^+(S) = \max_{(jm)} \left(Q_7(jm)\right).$$

In generating the various types of schedules, we shall describe the corresponding scheduling rule.

<u>Semi-active schedules</u>. A semi-active schedule can be generated by selecting an operation at random directly from the set of schedulable operations {s} regardless of any particular machine. Such an operation is scheduled as soon as possible. Specifically, select an operation $(j_0 m_0)$ at random such that $(j_0 m_0) \in \{s\}$. This procedure may be referred to as a semi-active scheduling rule.

For example, Table 4.4, which displays the initial scheduling table of our sample problem, shows that the initial set of schedulable operations, {s} contains operations (11) and (23), since $Q_3(11) = Q_3(23) = 0$. Operation (11) is selected by random for scheduling. Consequently, we set $Q_3(11) = -1$ and $Q_5(11) = 1$ to indicate that operation (11) has been scheduled on machine 1 first. The completion time of operation (11) is

$$Q_7(11) = Q_6(11) + Q_4(11) = 0 + 2 = 2.$$

Since operation (13) directly succeeds operation (11) as indicated in $Q_2(11)$, it cannot be started before the completion of operation (13) becomes

$$Q_6'(13) = \max \left(Q_6(13), Q_7(11)\right) = \max [0, 2] = 2.$$

We set $Q_3(13) = 0$ to indicate that operation (13) is now available for scheduling.

The updated set of schedulable operations contains (13) and (23). Since operation (13) is selected randomly for scheduling, we set $Q_3(13) = -1$ and

$Q_5(13) = 1$ to indicate that operation (13) has been scheduled on machine 3 first. Then, the completion time of operation (13) is

$$Q_7(13) = Q_6(13) + Q_4(13) = 2 + 4 = 6.$$

As operation (12) directly succeeds operation (13), the potential starting time of operation (12) becomes

$$Q_6(12) = \max \left(Q_6(12), Q_7(13)\right) = \max [0, 6] = 6.$$

In setting $Q_3(12) = 0$, the updated set of schedulable operations contains operations (12) and (23).

Following the semi-active scheduling rule, the remaining operations are assigned in the sequence (23), (21), (22), and (12). Consequently, a semi-active schedule with a schedule time of 19 is generated. The schedule which is displayed in Table 4.5 coincides with the Gantt chart of S_6 in Figure 4.6.

Table 4.4 Initial Scheduling Table of the (2x3) Job-Shop Sample Problem

Q_1	Q_2	Q_3	Q_4	Q_5	Q_6	Q_7
11	13	0	2			
21	22	1	4			
12		1	1			
22		1	5			
13	12	1	4			
23	21	0	3			

Table 4.5 Final Scheduling Table of Semi-Active Schedule S_6

Q_1	Q_2	Q_3	Q_4	Q_5	Q_6	Q_7
11	13	-1	2	1	0	2
21	22	-1	4	2	9	13
12		-1	1	2	18	19*
22		-1	5	1	13	18
13	12	-1	4	1	2	6
23	21	-1	3	2	6	9

Active Schedules. An active schedule can be generated by first partitioning the set of schedulable operations {s} by machine into M subsets $\{s_m\}$, m = 1, 2, ..., M. A subset on a particular machine is selected such that the associated operations, if scheduled, would be completed soonest. Within such a subset the operations are considered to be in conflict. A conflict is said to exist when there are two or more jobs to be performed on the same machine during a common time interval. An operation is selected at random from this subset to be scheduled as soon as possible. Thus, the conflict is said to be resolved in favor of that operation. This particular procedure may be referred to as an active scheduling rule.

As an illustration, we examine the initial scheduling table of our sample problem displayed in Table 4.4. The initial set of schedulable operations {s} contains (11) and (23). This set is partitioned by machine into M or 3 subsets such that

$$\{s_1\} = (11), \qquad \{s_2\} = \phi, \qquad \{s_3\} = (23) .$$

Note that at this stage, the subset $\{s_2\}$ is empty, since it has no schedulable operations on machine 2. Operation (11) is selected to be scheduled, since it would be completed earlier than operation (23). Thus, the completion time of operation (11) is $Q_7(11) = 2$. As operation (13) directly succeeds operation (11), its potential starting time becomes $Q_6(13) = 2$.

The updated set of schedulable operations contains operations (13) and (23) which have machine 3 in common. Thus the subsets $\{s_m\}$, m = 1, 2, 3 are such that

$$\{s_1\} = \phi, \qquad \{s_2\} = \phi, \qquad \{s_3\} = (13), (23) .$$

This indicates that there is a conflict between jobs 1 and 2 on machine 3. Consequently, operation (13) is selected randomly to be scheduled. The completion time of operation (13) is $Q_7(13) = 6$. The potential starting time of operation (12) is $Q_6(12) = 6$, since it directly succeeds operation (13) which has been scheduled.

At this stage the updated set of schedulable operations {s} contains operations (12) and (23). When this set is partitioned by machine, the resulting subsets are

$$\{s_1\} = \phi, \qquad \{s_2\} = (12), \qquad \{s_3\} = (23) .$$

There is no conflict between operations (12) and (23), since both operations have no common machine. We select operation (12) because it would be completed earlier.

Thus, the completion time of operation (12) is $Q_7(12) = 7$. Next, the updated set of schedulable operations contains operations (21) and (23).

When the remaining operations are assigned in the sequence (23), (21), and (22) according to the active scheduling rule, the result is an active schedule, displayed in Table 4.6, with a schedule time of 18. This is the schedule S_8 whose Gantt chart is shown in Figure 4.6.

Table 4.6 Final Scheduling Table of Active Schedule S_8

Q_1	Q_2	Q_3	Q_4	Q_5	Q_6	Q_7
11	13	-1	2	1	0	2
21	22	-1	4	2	9	13
12		-1	1	1	6	7
22		-1	5	2	13	18*
13	12	-1	4	1	2	6
23	21	-1	3	2	6	9

Table 4.7 Final Scheduling Table of Non-delay Schedule S_4

Q_1	Q_2	Q_3	Q_4	Q_5	Q_6	Q_7
11	13	-1	2	1	0	2
21	22	-1	4	2	3	7
12		-1	1	1	7	8
22		-1	5	2	8	13*
13	12	-1	4	2	3	7
23	21	-1	3	1	0	3

<u>Non-delay schedules</u>. A non-delay schedule can be generated by first partitioning the set of schedulable operations $\{s\}$ into M subsets, $\{s_m\}$, $m = 1, 2, \ldots, M$. These subsets are reduced to subsets $\{s_m^*\}$ to include only those operations for which the earliest starting time s_{jm} is less than or equal to the earliest machine availability time a_m. An operation is selected from the subset $\{s_m^*\}$ to be scheduled as soon as possible. This selection may be made according to one of the following rules: (1) select the operation that has been waiting longest at the particular machine; (2) select the operation that has the shortest processing time on that machine and

break the tie, if any, by the first rule; (3) select the operation that has the most remaining processing time to completion and break the tie, if any, by the first rule; or (4) select the operation at random. This procedure may be referred to as non-delay scheduling rule.

As an illustration, the initial scheduling table displayed in Table 4.4 shows that the set of the schedulable operations contains operations (11) and (23). This set is partitioned by machine into three subsets $\{s_m\}$, m = 1, 2, 3. Since starting times of both operations and the availability time of machines 1 and 3 are zero, the subsets $\{s_m^*\}$ are such that

$$\{s_1^*\} = (11), \qquad \{s_2^*\} = \phi, \qquad \{s_3^*\} = (23).$$

Operation (11) is selected because it has the shortest processing time. The computation proceeds as before. The updated set of schedulable operations contains operations (13) and (23). The earliest starting times of both operations s_{13} and s_{23} are 2 and 0, respectively. The earliest availability time of machine 3 is $a_3 = 0$. Thus, we select operation (23) to be scheduled. The completion time of operation (23) is $Q_7(23) = 3$. As operation (21) directly succeeds operation (23), its potential starting time becomes $Q_6(21) = 3$. The updated set of schedulable operations, at this stage, contains operations (13) and (21). Both operations are scheduled at the same time, since the corresponding machines are different.

Finally, the updated set of schedulable operations contain operations (12) and (22). The potential starting time of both operations is $s_{12} = s_{22} = 7$, and the available time of machine 2 is $a_2 = 7$. Thus, the subset $\{s_2^*\}$ contains operations (12) and (22). If the shortest processing time rule is applied to break the tie, operation (12) would precede operation (22). The result is a non-delay schedule displayed in Table 4.7. However, if the most remaining processing time to completion rule is applied, operation (22) would precede operation (12). Thus, the result would be another non-delay schedule. Both schedules are shown in Figure 4.6 as S_4 and S_2, respectively.

The idea of generating active and non-delay schedules can be presented in a compact form. An active schedule is generated if the next operation is selected by the rule

$$\min \left[\min_{(jm)\varepsilon\{s_m\}} \left[\max \left(a_m, s_{jm} \right) + t_{jm} \right] \right],$$

and a non-delay schedule is generated if the next operation is selected by the rule

$$\min \left[\min_{(jm)\varepsilon\{s_m\}} \left[\max \left(a_m, s_{jm} \right) \right] \right],$$

where

a_m earliest availability time of machine m,

a_{jm} earliest starting time of job j on machine m.

The reader is encouraged to apply the above rules in generating the active and non-delay schedules displayed in Figure 4.6.

Analysis of Schedules

Our next task is to study the properties of schedules with regard to a certain measure of performance, in particular, the schedule time. First, we carry out the analysis by developing various lower and upper bounds on the schedule time as a function of processing times. We pursue the matter a step further by deriving two estimates of the number of distinct schedule times: one as a function of processing times, and the other as a function of the number of jobs and machines. These interesting results establish the fact that there are many schedules that yield the same schedule time. In other words, the number of distinct schedule times is much smaller than the number of schedules.

<u>Bounds on schedule times</u>. To facilitate the analysis, we shall assume that the processing times of the various operations are non-negative integers. As a result, the schedule time becomes an integer. An expression for the upper bound on the schedule time can be found such that

$$c^+(S) \leq \sum_{j=1}^{J} \sum_{\ell=1}^{M} t_{jm_\ell},$$

where we would have strict equality, if there are no simultaneous operations on the machines.

Various lower bounds on the schedule time can be obtained. Finding an exact value of the minimum schedule time; however, seems as difficult as developing an efficient procedure for the sequence which has the optimal schedule time. A lower bound on the schedule time can be expressed such that

$$c^+(S) \geq \max_{m_\ell} \left(\sum_{j=1}^{J} t_{jm_\ell} \right),$$

since all jobs are performed individually on each of the machines. The above estimate of the minimum schedule time is simply obtained by first summing the processing times of all jobs on each machine. The maximum of these values is the lower bound. We would expect strict equality, if there were no idle times on the machine which has the maximum total processing time. This estimate can be strengthened for both flow- and job-shop problems, independently.

In flow-shop problems in which all jobs have the same flow pattern, the lower bound on the schedule time is given such that

$$c^+(S) \geq \max_{m} \left(\sum_{j'=1}^{J} t_{j'm} \right) + \min_{j} \left(\sum_{m'=1}^{m-1} t_{jm'} \right) + \min_{\hat{j} \neq j} \left(\sum_{m'=m+1}^{M} t_{\hat{j}m'} \right),$$

where m in the second and third sums is that m giving the maximum in the first term; and j in the third sum is that j giving the minimum in the second term. The above estimate states that the minimum schedule time cannot be shorter than the total processing time for all jobs on machine m plus the shortest time of processing, say, job j, on machines 1, 2, ..., m-1 plus the shortest time of processing, say, job $\hat{j}$ on machines m+1, m+2, ..., M, where clearly job j must be different than job $\hat{j}$.

We would expect strict equality in the above estimate, if (1) there were no idle times on machine m after processing the first operation on this machine, $(j_1 m)$; (2) the sequence relations are such that the second sum is the total processing times of jobs on machines m+1, m+2, ..., M after the last operation on machine m, $(j_J m)$ has been processed. On the other hand, we would expect strict inequality, if there were idle times on machine m. In such a case, the difference between the minimum schedule time and the lower bound measures, in a way, the loss of time caused by the necessity of fitting jobs into the time available on machines.

For illustration, consider a flow-shop problem having six jobs and three machines. The corresponding processing time matrix is shown as follows:

$$T = \begin{pmatrix} 6 & 7 & 3 \\ 12 & 2 & 3 \\ 4 & 6 & 8 \\ 3 & 11 & 7 \\ 6 & 8 & 10 \\ 2 & 14 & 12 \end{pmatrix}.$$

All jobs are processed on machine 1 first, machine 2 second, and machine 3 last. The sum of processing times of all jobs on machine 2 gives the maximum of 48. The minimum processing times on machines 1 and 3 are 2 and 3, respectively. Thus, the lower bound on the schedule time becomes

$$c^+(S) \geq 48 + 2 + 3$$

or

$$c^+(S) \geq 53.$$

The above flow-shop problem has a minimum schedule time of 57. Note that as the number of machines increases, the lower bound becomes a poor estimate of the optimal schedule time.

Because of several deficiencies in the above lower bound, an alternative lower bound is expressed such that

$$c^+(S) \geq \max\left\{\max_j\left(\sum_{m'=1}^{M} t_{jm'}\right), \max_m\left[\min_j\left(\sum_{m'=1}^{m-1} t_{jm'}\right) + \sum_{j=1}^{J} t_{jm} + \min_j\left(\sum_{m'=m+1}^{M} t_{jm'}\right)\right]\right\},$$

where j giving the minimum in the first term may be the same j giving the minimum in the third term, which is not so in the former lower bound. Using the above (6x3) flow-shop problem, the modified lower bound is

$$c^+(S) \geq \max\left\{28, \max\begin{pmatrix} 0 + 33 + 5 \\ 2 + 48 + 3 \\ 10 + 43 \end{pmatrix}\right\},$$

or

$$c^+(S) \geq 53.$$

Note that in some instances, the modified lower bound is more powerful, since it may be greater than or equal to the former lower bound.

The former lower bound is deficient in three respects. To discuss and illustrate these deficiencies, consider three flow-shop problems, each with two jobs and three machines. The associated processing time matrices are shown as follows:

$$T_1 = \begin{pmatrix} 6 & 5 & 3 \\ 1 & 3 & 2 \end{pmatrix}, \quad T_2 = \begin{pmatrix} 2 & 1 & 4 \\ 1 & 5 & 3 \end{pmatrix}, \quad T_3 = \begin{pmatrix} 2 & 1 & 4 \\ 1 & 5 & 1 \end{pmatrix}.$$

The three deficiencies are listed in the following:

1. In some cases, the total processing time of a particular job on all machines dominates the lower bound. For example, in problem 1 the former lower bound is 12; however, the total processing time of job 1 on all machines is 14. The modified lower bound is 14 which is the minimum schedule time.

2. In some other cases, a particular machine may be more critical than that with the maximum processing times. For example, in problem 2 the former lower bound is 10; however, the modified lower bound is 11 which is the minimum schedule time.

3. In certain cases, a higher value than the former lower bound can be obtained, if the same job is allowed to provide both the second and third term. For example, in problem 3 the former lower bound is 11, but the modified lower bound is 8. The minimum schedule time in this case is 9.

It should be pointed out that both lower bounds have been computed for 400 problems of different sizes. The associated processing times have been generated from a uniform distribution between one and 30, inclusive. The computational results reveal that there are no significant differences between the values of both lower bounds. Thus, we can conclude that the above three problems are quite extreme cases.

In job-shop problems in which each job has a different flow pattern, the lower bound on the schedule time may be expressed such that

$$c^+(S) \geq \max \left[\max_j \left(\sum_{\ell=1}^{M} t_{jm_\ell} \right), \max_{m_\delta} \left(\sum_{j=1}^{J} \sum_{\ell=1}^{M} t_{jm_\ell} \Delta_{jm_\delta} \right) \right]$$

where

$$\Delta_{jm_\delta} = \begin{cases} 1, & \text{if job } j \text{ is processed on machine } m_\delta, \\ 0, & \text{otherwise.} \end{cases}$$

This lower bound is simply the overall maximum of both the total processing time for each job and the total processing time on each machine. Note that in the case where each job has a different number of operations, M is replaced by M_j to denote the number of operations for job j.

For illustration, consider the job-shop sample problem which we have been using. For convenience, the machine ordering and processing time matrices are reproduced below:

$$M = \begin{pmatrix} 11 & 13 & 12 \\ 23 & 21 & 22 \end{pmatrix}, \quad T = \begin{pmatrix} 2 & 4 & 1 \\ 3 & 4 & 5 \end{pmatrix}.$$

The lower bound on the schedule time is

$$c^+(S) \geq \max \left[\max \begin{Bmatrix} 2+4+1 \\ 3+4+5 \end{Bmatrix}, \max \begin{pmatrix} (2)(1) + (4)(1) \\ (1)(1) + (5)(1) \\ (4)(1) + (3)(1) \end{pmatrix} \right]$$

or

$$c^+(S) \geq 12.$$

However, upon examining the various schedules of this problem displayed in Figure 4.6, it appears that the minimum schedule time is 13.

<u>Number of distinct schedule times</u>. An interesting study conducted by Heller [12] shows that there are many semi-active schedules that yield the same schedule time. In other words, the number of the distinct schedule times is very small compared to the number of the semi-active schedules. We shall consider two estimates of the number of distinct schedule times. One estimate makes use of the fact that if the processing times are integer numbers, the schedule time is also an integer. The other estimate is purely combinatorial as it depends on the number of jobs and machines. The results of these estimates are rather central to the study of the statistical aspects of scheduling with which Chapter 5 is concerned.

A simple estimate of the number of distinct schedule times can be obtained as a function of processing times by considering both the maximum and minimum schedule times. Assuming that all processing times are integers, all schedule times can take on integer values between these bounds. Thus, an upper bound on the number of distinct schedule times N_d is

$$N_d \leq c^+(S^+) - c^+(S^*) + 1,$$

where

$c^+(S^+)$ maximum schedule time, or upper bound on the schedule time,
$c^+(S^*)$ minimum schedule time, or lower bound on the schedule time.

Note that there is no loss of generality in assuming that all processing times are integer values, since these processing times can always be multiplied by a suitable constant so that they become integers. The upper and lower bounds on the schedule time presented earlier for both flow- and job-shop problems can be used to compute a simple crude upper bound on the number of distinct schedule times.

Another simple estimate can be obtained as a function of the number of jobs and machines. Since a schedule time is a sum over a subset of JM processing times (JM operations, each having a processing time), an upper bound on the number of distinct schedule times can be obtained by counting the number of possible terms that appear in the sum behind the total completion time for all schedules. The least number of these terms is J+M-1, which is obtained when all jobs have the same machine ordering. Whereas, the maximum number of terms is JM, which occurs when there is no simultaneous operation. Thus, if all processing times are different, an upper bound on the number of distinct schedule times would be the number of different possible sums. This leads to the following. For job-shop problems in which the processing times are different, an upper bound on the number of distinct schedule times is

$$N_d \leq \sum_{n=J+M-1}^{JM} \binom{JM}{n} ,$$

or

$$N_d \leq 2^{JM} - \sum_{n=0}^{J+M-2} \binom{JM}{n} ,$$

where clearly J and M are the numbers of jobs and machines, respectively.

When all jobs have the same machine ordering, there are only J+M-1 terms. This leads to the following. For job-shop problems in which the processing times are different, an upper bound on the number of distinct schedule times is

$$N_d \leq \binom{JM}{J+M-1} .$$

Table 4.8 displays the different numbers of possible sequences and distinct schedule times for flow-shop and job-shop problems of varied numbers of jobs and machines.

An immediate consequence of the above analysis is to attempt to study the probability distribution of the schedule times. The statistical aspects of scheduling will then be discussed in the succeeding chapter.

Table 4.8 Numbers of Possible Sequences and Distinct Schedule Times

Number of Jobs	Number of Machines	Number of Possible Sequences	Number of Distinct Schedule Times Flow-Shop	Number of Distinct Schedule Times Job-Shop
2	3	0.80×10	1.50×10	2.20×10
	4	1.60×10	5.60×10	9.30×10
	5	3.20×10	2.10×10^2	3.86×10^2
3	3	2.16×10^2	1.26×10^2	2.56×10^2
	4	1.30×10^3	9.24×10^2	2.51×10^3
	5	7.78×10^3	6.44×10^3	2.28×10^4
4	3	1.38×10^4	9.24×10^2	2.51×10^3
	4	3.32×10^5	1.14×10^4	5.06×10^4
	5	7.96×10^6	1.26×10^5	9.11×10^5
5	3	1.73×10^6	6.44×10^3	2.28×10^4
	4	2.07×10^8	1.26×10^5	9.11×10^5
	5	2.49×10^{10}	2.04×10^6	3.17×10^7
6	3	3.73×10^8	4.38×10^4	1.99×10^5
	4	2.69×10^{11}	1.31×10^6	1.55×10^7
	5	1.93×10^{14}	3.00×10^7	1.05×10^9
8	3	6.55×10^{13}	1.96×10^6	1.42×10^7
	4	2.64×10^{18}	1.29×10^8	4.19×10^9
	5	1.06×10^{23}	5.59×10^9	1.09×10^{13}
10	3	4.78×10^{19}	8.65×10^7	9.66×10^8
	4	1.73×10^{26}	1.20×10^{10}	1.09×10^{12}
	5	6.29×10^{32}	9.38×10^{11}	1.13×10^{15}

REFERENCES

[1] Akers, S. B. and J. Friedman, "A Non-Numerical Approach to Production Scheduling Problems," <u>Operations Research</u>, Vol. 3, No. 4, 1955, pp. 429-442.

[2] Ashour, S., "A Decomposition Approach for the Machine Scheduling Problem," Ph.D. Thesis, University of Iowa, Iowa City, Iowa, 1967.

[3] Ashour, S., "A Decomposition Approach for the Machine Scheduling Problem," <u>The International Journal of Production Research</u>, Vol. 6, No. 2, 1967, pp. 109-122.

[4] Ashour, S., "Combinatorial Analysis of JxM Sequencing Problems," presented before the 34th National Meeting of the Operations Research Society of America, Philadelphia, Pennsylvania, November 6-9, 1968.

[5] Ashour, S., "Graph-Theoretic Approach to Flow Shop Scheduling Problems," <u>Production and Inventory Management</u>, 4-th Qtr., 1969.

[6] Bakshi, M. S. and S. R. Arora, "The Machine Sequencing Problem," <u>Management Science</u>, Vol. 16, No. 4, 1969, pp. B247-263.

[7] Conway, R. W., W. L. Maxwell and L. W. Miller, <u>Theory of Scheduling</u>, Addison-Wesley Publishing Company, Reading, Massachusetts, 1967, pp. 80-83 and 109-117.

[8] Fisher, H. and G. L. Thompson, "Probabilistic Learning Combinations of Local Job-Shop Scheduling Rules," Chapter 15 in *Industrial Scheduling*, (eds. J. F. Muth and G. L. Thompson), Prentic-Hall Inc., Englewood Cliffs, New Jersey, 1963.

[9] Gere, W. S. Jr., "A Heuristic Approach to Job Shop Scheduling," Ph.D. Thesis, Carnegie Institute of Technology, Pittsburgh, Pennsylvania, 1962.

[10] Giffler, B. and G. L. Thompson, "Algorithms for Solving Production Scheduling Problems," *Operations Research*, Vol. 8, No. 4, 1960, pp. 487-503.

[11] Giffler, B., G. L. Thompson and V. VanNess, "Numerical Experience with the Linear and Monte Carlo Algorithms for Solving Production Scheduling Problems," Chapter 3 in *Industrial Scheduling*, (eds. J. F. Muth and G. L. Thompson), Prentice-Hall Inc., Englewood Cliffs, New Jersey, 1963.

[12] Heller, J., "Combinatorial, Probabilistic and Statistical Aspects of an (MxJ) Scheduling Problem," Report NYO-2540, AEC Computed and Applied Mathematics Center, Institute of Mathematical Science, New York University, New York, N.Y., February 1959.

[13] Heller, J., "Combinatorial Properties of Machine Shop Scheduling," Report NYO-2879, AEC Computed and Applied Mathematics Center, Institute of Mathematical Science, New York University, New York, N.Y., July 1959.

[14] Heller, J. and G. Logemann, "An Algorithm for the Construction and Evaluation of Feasible Schedules," *Management Science*, Vol. 8, No. 2, 1962, pp. 168-183.

[15] Marimont, R. B., "A New Method of Checking the Consistency of Precedence Matrices," *Journal of the Association for Computing Machinery*, Vol. 6, No. 2, 1959, pp. 164-171.

[16] Nelson, R. T., "Job Shop Scheduling: An Application of Linear Programming," Report RR-28, Management Sciences Research Project, University of California at Los Angeles, Los Angeles, California, March 1954.

[17] Nelson, R. T., "Enumeration of a Three Job, Three Machine Scheduling Problem on SWAC," Report DP-50, Management Sciences Research Project, University of California at Los Angeles, Los Angeles, California, January 1955.

[18] Nugent, C. E., "On Sampling Approaches to the Solution of the n-by-m Static Sequencing Problem," Ph.D. Thesis, Cornell University, Ithaca, New York, 1964.

CHAPTER 5

STATISTICAL ASPECTS

Our treatment of the shop scheduling problem in the preceding chapter has been combinatorial in character. Because of the tremendous number of schedules involved and the fact that the number of distinct schedule times is much smaller than the number of schedules, sampling from the set of semi-active schedules has elicited a great deal of theoretical study [3, 7, 9, 12, 14]. Each of these studies has essentially been the application of particular rules or procedures to generate a subset of schedules with certain properties. The characteristics of schedules in each subset determine the form of the conditional distribution of schedule values. Certainly, some conditional distribution is likely to be preferable to the others. For example, if one were to seek a good schedule from a randomly generated set of schedules, it would be more efficient to sample from a conditional distribution in which a heavier mass of schedules is very close to the optimal. Sampling from such a distribution would increase the probability of selecting good schedules while decreasing the probability of selecting others.

The purpose of this chapter is to investigate the statistical characteristics of schedule times. This is accomplished by first sampling various subsets of schedules each with certain properties and then studying the forms of the associated schedule time distributions. We shall report on two theoretical studies. The first study is concerned with fitting the normal distribution to the schedule times whose schedules are generated directly from the set of semi-active schedules [10, 12]. The other study is concerned with the statistical effects of decomposition schedule times [1, 3]. These schedule times are obtained by decomposing a set of jobs into a number of subsets, each of which is scheduled independently. An interesting feature of this study is that the schedule time distribution shifts toward the optimal as the number of jobs in each subset increases.

5.1 Theoretical Study I

As a prelude to the statistical study of the schedule times over a set of schedules, the following observation is rather fundamental. In spite of the existence of a very large number of schedules, there is much smaller number of distinct schedule times for any given set of processing times. As a consequence of this observation, the number of distinct schedule times has been estimated in Section 4.2. To illustrate this observation, consider the (6x3) flow-shop problem, presented in Section 4.2, which has the following processing time matrix:

$$T = \begin{pmatrix} 6 & 7 & 3 \\ 12 & 2 & 3 \\ 4 & 6 & 8 \\ 3 & 11 & 7 \\ 6 & 8 & 10 \\ 2 & 14 & 12 \end{pmatrix}$$

In applying Theorem II of Section 4.1, it is sufficient to investigate only the permutation schedules. The 6! or 720 permutation schedules are enumerated. The corresponding schedule times are easily found by the use of a Gantt chart or a computer. The schedule times are then arranged in ascending order. The frequencies of the distinct schedule times are obtained and displayed in Table 5.1. In examining this frequency table, it appears that there are only 22 distinct schedule times obtained from the 720 alternative schedules. For a graphic presentation of the frequency table, the corresponding frequency distribution is plotted as shown in Figure 5.1.

Table 5.1 Frequency Table of Schedule Times Obtained by Complete Enumeration for a (6x3) Flow-Shop Problem

Schedule Time	Frequency	Schedule Time	Frequency
57	3	69	31
59	92	70	24
60	37	71	29
61	37	72	31
62	41	73	21
63	50	74	22
64	60	75	7
65	45	76	24
66	45	77	3
67	59	78	6
68	51	80	2

This observation would lead immediately to the following conclusion. For a large number of jobs with any set of processing times, one would expect to approximate the histogram of Figure 5.1 by some theoretical probability distribution function. The parameters of such a distribution can be estimated by any sampling technique. Along this line, Heller [10,11,12] has conducted a number of numerical experiments for flow-shop problems in which all jobs have the same machine ordering. The investigation is two-fold: (1) study the form of the schedule time distribution over all possible schedules; and (2) suggest a sampling procedure for the probable determination of a best schedule. We shall report on Heller's four numerical experiments.

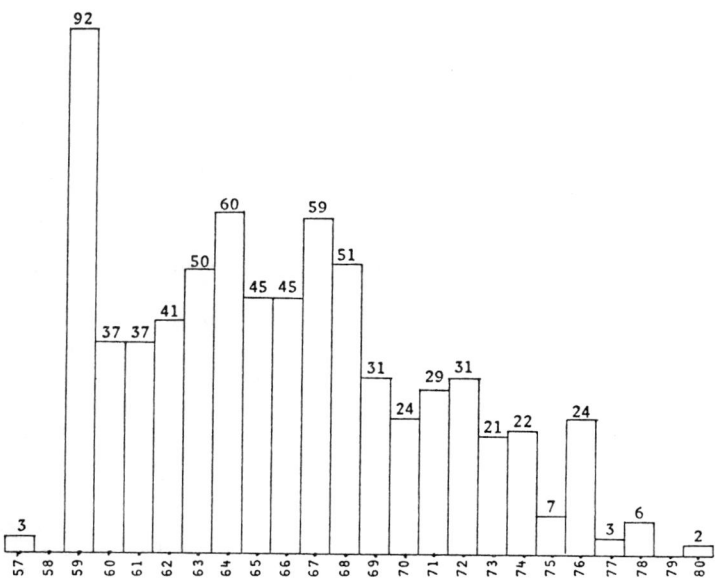

Figure 5.1. Frequency Distribution of Schedule Times For a (6x3) Flow-Shop Sample Problem

In all the experiments an integer processing time for each job on each machine is generated from a uniform distribution with certain intervals. Two different sets of schedules are considered: (1) a set of schedules with common job sequencings (or a set of permutation schedules); and (2) a set of schedules with independent job sequencings. A schedule with common job sequencings is generated by selecting J random numbers uniformly distributed between 0 and 1. The J jobs are then ranked according to the values of the corresponding random numbers. The resulting job sequencing is applied to all machines and the overall sequence is evaluated to obtain the associated schedule time. On the other hand, a schedule with independent job sequencings is generated by repeating the above process for each machine independently. The result in each case yields one overall sequence whose schedule time can be obtained.

In generating a number of schedules, no attempt has been made to check if any schedule has been previously produced, that is, sampling is with replacement. In each experiment the schedules obtained are ordered and the frequency of the distinct schedule times are obtained. Consequently, the empirical frequency distribution of the distinct schedule times is plotted. Now, we exhibit the pertinent data and results of the four experiments.

Sampling Experiment I. The first experiment involves a set of 100 jobs to be processed on 10 machines. The processing times are generated from a uniform distribution with the interval [0,9]. The sample size is 3,000 permutation schedules. Figure 5.2 depicts some of the sample probabilities versus the schedule times.

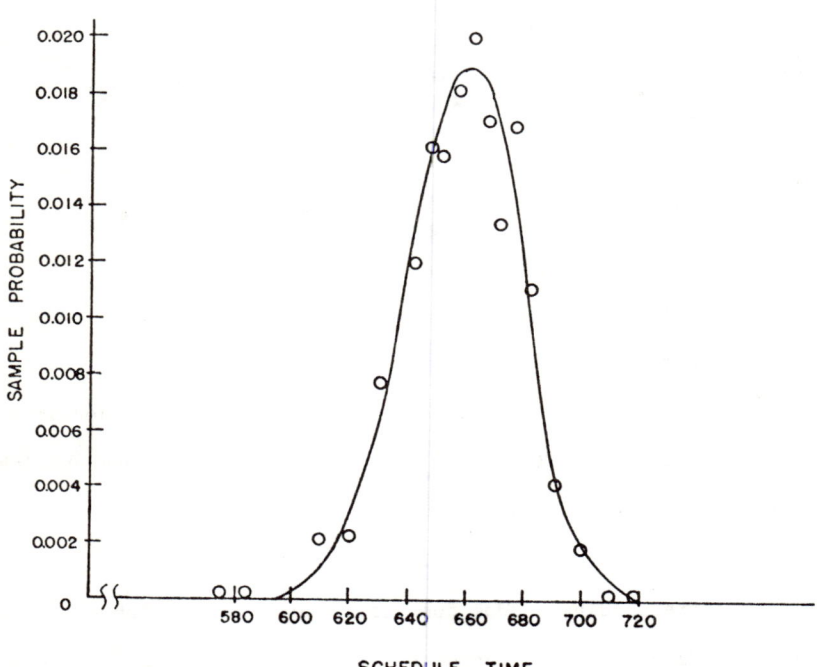

Figure 5.2. Schedule Time Sample Distribution for Experiment I
(Heller [10])

A normal distribution function having a sample mean of 656.81, sample variance of 20.80, and range of 606 to 707 is fitted to the resulting empirical frequency distribution. As shown in Figure 5.2, it is only near the tails of the distribution that the sampling has failed to find some schedule times.

Sampling Experiment II. The second experiment consists of a set of 20 jobs to be performed on 10 machines. The processing times are those of the first 20 jobs in Experiment I. Two sampling procedures are carried out, one is to produce a set of 12,000 schedules with common job sequencings and the other is to produce a set of 9,037 schedules with independent job sequencings. The sample distributions of schedule times for both sets of schedules are shown in Figure 5.3. The sample

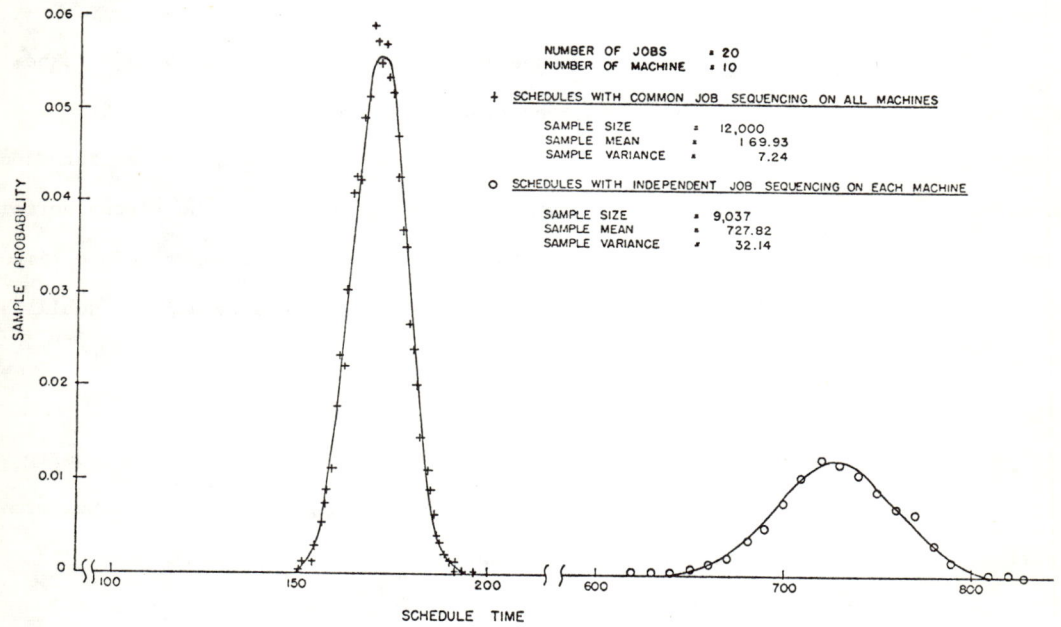

Figure 5.3 Schedule Time Sample Distribution for Experiment II
(Heller [10])

distribution obtained from those schedules which have common job sequencing on all machines that all integer values of schedule times exist between the minimum and maximum sample schedule times except for one value at the upper tail of the distribution.

It is apparent from Figure 5.3 that both sample distributions are entirely non-overlapping. The maximum schedule time observed for the set of schedules with common job sequencings is much smaller than the minimum schedule times observed for the set of schedules with independent job sequencings. As Conway et. al. [5] have pointed out, the reason for this non-overlapping can be easily seen by examining a schedule with independent job sequencing on each machine. Consider the machine m which determines the schedule time of that schedule. Let job a be in the first sequence-position on machine m. Consequently, job a is equally likely to be in any one of the J or 20 sequence-positions on machine m-1. Machine m cannot perform any other job until job a has been completed on machine m-1. It is possible to have as many as J-1 or 19 jobs completed on machine m-1 and waiting to be processed on machine m. Thus, each machine cannot start processing until its predecessor has completed, on the average, half its work load.

Sampling Experiment III. The third experiment involves a set of 20 jobs to be processed on 10 machines. In this case, the processing times are generated from a uniform distribution with the interval [1,99]. The sample size is 10,000 permutation schedules. Figure 5.4 depicts some of the sample probabilities and the fitted normal distribution function. As we might expect, the sample variance of the schedule times is larger than those in the previous experiments. Because of the relatively small sample size, the fitting of the normal distribution to the empirical frequency distribution is somewhat poor.

Sampling Experiment IV. The fourth experiment consists of a set of 30 jobs to be performed on 5 machines. The processing times are again generated from a uniform distribution but with the interval [3,997]. The sample size is 11,250 permutation schedules. As seen in Figure 5.5, a very poor fitting between both the empirical and theoretical normal distributions is obvious. It has been claimed that the reason for that is the wide spread of the processing times and the relatively small sample size.

Heller [13] has concluded that the above numerical experiments show that the distribution of schedule times is normal; the theroretical analysis indicates that the schedule times are asymptotically normally distributed over schedules having large numbers of jobs and with any given set of processing times. This theoretical analysis is based on an approximation to the central limit theorem for a particular

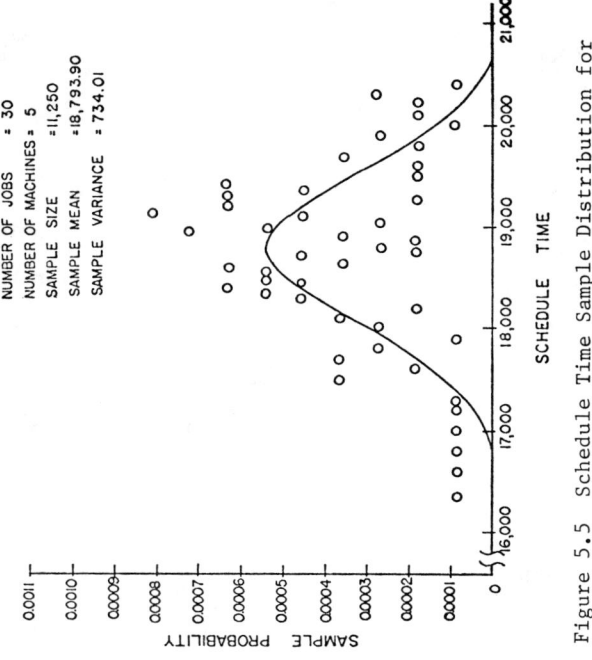

Figure 5.5 Schedule Time Sample Distribution for Experiment IV (Heller [10])

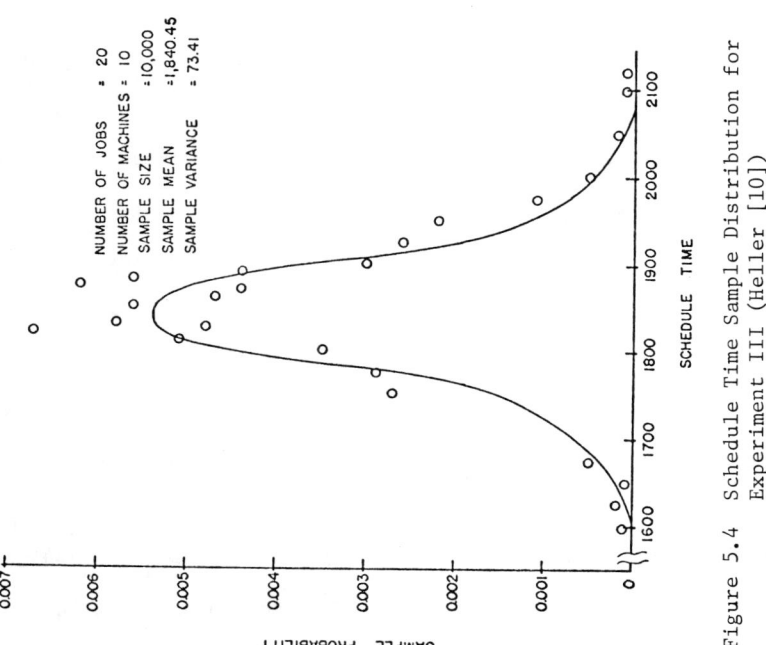

Figure 5.4 Schedule Time Sample Distribution for Experiment III (Heller [10])

periodic Markov-chain. Sampling from such a distribution is inconceivable because of two reasons. First, the departures from normality are most pronounced in the tails of the distribution; it is clear that the lower tail of the distribution is the area of interest. Second, more efficient distributions are available to sample from.

5.2 Theoretical Study II

We now study the effects of decomposition on the forms of schedule time distributions. The decomposition procedure consists of partitioning a set of jobs into a series of smaller subsets. The minimum schedule times obtained for these subsets are combined to form a schedule time overall the original set of jobs. The procedure followed by a sample problem will be discussed below.

Consider a set of J jobs, $\{s\} = \{j | 1 \leq j \leq J$ and $J \neq$ a prime number$\}$, decompose the set $\{s\}$, in all possible ways, into G mutually exclusive subsets, $\{s_g\}$, $1 \leq g \leq G$ such that the subset consists of K jobs with $K = J/G$, where K and G are positive integers. Note that the number of jobs in each subset is the same. This can be accomplished, in a systematic fashion, by constructing all distinguishable arrangements of J jobs involving G subsets, each having K jobs. The number of such arrangements is $R = J!/(k!)^G$. No attention is paid to the sequence of the jobs in each subset. Within each arrangement and for each subset, the sequence which yields the minimum schedule time is obtained. The resulting schedule times associated with these sequences are then combined to obtain the schedule time over all the J jobs. In combining the schedule times within each arrangement, the idle times are utilized, if possible, between each two successive subsets. This procedure is repeated for all possible arrangements and the minimum schedule time is observed. This minimum value is the decomposition solution with K equaling a number of jobs such that $1 \leq K \leq J$.

It is intuitively obvious that one must simultaneously schedule the J jobs when the number of subsets is equal to the number of jobs, or $G = J$, and consequently, each subset consists of one job, or $K = 1$. This is the procedure discussed in Section 5.1. However, it will be referred to herein as decomposition with $K = 1$. Incidentally, in the above case, the form of the schedule time distribution, as shown in the preceding section, is asympototically normal.

It is also clear that any schedule time over a set of J jobs obtained by decomposition with 1 < K < J (intermediate cases) is a result of combining the sequences, within each arrangement, having the minimum schedule times. The other sequences are certainly discarded. Thus, one would conjecture that the distribution of the combined schedule times shifts toward the optimal. Furthermore, in fitting the schedule times of the sequences within each arrangement there are idle times on the various machines between each two successive subsets. The amount of these idle times decreases, and hence the combined schedule time becomes shorter as the number of subsets decreases or as the number of jobs in each subset increases. An implication of the above is that the amount of distribution shift becomes larger as the number of jobs in each subset increases.

However, in the extreme case, when all J jobs are in one subset or G = 1, that is, K = J, the schedule time distribution becomes a point distribution with all the weight at the optimal value. Figure 5.6 shows the conjectured schedule time distributions which would be obtained by decomposition with K = 1, 2, 3, and 6 for a problem of six jobs and an arbitrary number of machines.

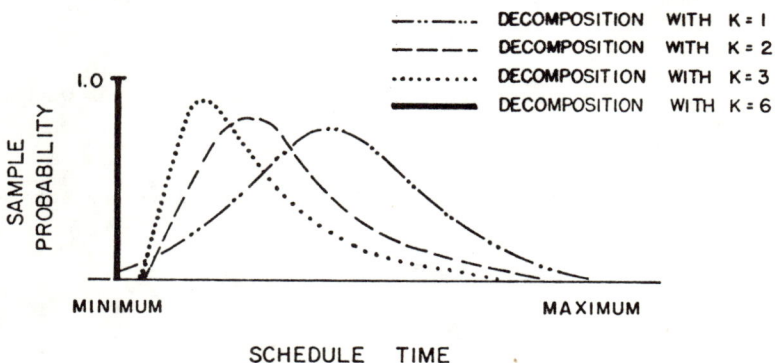

Figure 5.6. Conjectured Schedule Time Distributions Obtained by Decomposition

The above conjectures, which are verified empirically, suggest that we would sample from one of the distributions obtained by decomposition with $1 < K \leq J$. For a particular sample size, the shift of the distributions obtained by decomposition with $1 < K \leq J$ should increase the probability of determining an optimal solution. An obvious corrollary to the above would be that for a given probability of obtaining an optimal solution, we should require a smaller sample size when sampling from one of the decomposition distributions with $1 < K \leq J$ than sampling from a decomposition distribution with $K = 1$.

In order to grasp the idea of decomposition, let us consider the sample problem that we have been using in the preceding section. The notation that will be used is the following:

T_{gr} processing time matrix of subset g within arrangement r

M_{gr} machine ordering matrix of subset g within arrangement r

$c^+(S_{gr})$ schedule time associated with the sequence of subset g within arrangement r

s_{grm} starting time of jobs in subset g within arrangement r on machine m

c_{grm} completion time of jobs in subset g within arrangement r on machine m

δ_{grm} idle time g between two successive subsets within arrangement r on machine m

Δ_{gr} minimum idle time g between two successive subsets within arrangement r

$c^+(S_r)$ schedule time associated with the combined sequences within arrangement r.

For convenience, the processing time matrix of the (6x3) flow-shop sample problem is reproduced below:

$$T = \begin{pmatrix} 6 & 7 & 3 \\ 12 & 2 & 3 \\ 4 & 6 & 8 \\ 3 & 11 & 7 \\ 6 & 8 & 10 \\ 2 & 14 & 12 \end{pmatrix}$$

Four decomposition solutions can be obtained for the above sample problem.

<u>Decomposition with K = 6</u>. This decomposition solution is obtained by constructing 6!/6! or one arrangement of 6 jobs involving one subset. The sequence which yields the minimum schedule time is obtained by one of the available techniques. The optimal sequence yield a schedule time of 57. This value is the decomposition solution with

K = 6. Note that in such a case, the result is a degenerate distribution, since the probability of obtaining the optimal schedule time is one.

<u>Decomposition with K = 3</u>. This decomposition solution is obtained by first constructing the complete set of arrangements of 6 jobs involving 2 subsets, each having 3 jobs. The number of such arrangements is $R = 6!/(3!)^2$ or 20. These arrangements are displayed in Table 5.2. To find the schedule time associated with each of these arrangements, we shall proceed with the following steps. The computation is carried out; however, for the first arrangement only.

Table 5.2 Arrangements and Associated Schedule Times Obtained by Decomposition with K=3 for a (6x3) Flow-Shop Problem

Arrangement Number	Arrangement	Schedule Time	Arrangement Number	Arrangement	Schedule Time
1	1 2 3 4 5 6	67	11	2 3 4 1 5 6	62
2	1 2 4 3 5 6	65	12	2 3 5 1 4 6	60
3	1 2 5 3 4 5	67	13	2 3 6 1 4 5	60
4	1 2 6 3 4 5	60	14	2 4 5 1 3 6	64
5	1 3 4 2 5 6	67	15	2 4 6 1 3 5	59
6	1 3 5 2 4 6	61	16	2 5 6 1 3 4	62
7	1 3 6 2 4 5	63	17	3 4 5 1 2 6	61
8	1 4 5 2 3 6	64	18	3 4 6 1 2 5	59
9	1 4 6 2 3 5	61	19	3 5 6 1 2 4	57
10	1 5 6 2 3 4	62	20	4 5 6 1 2 3	62

Step 1. Set arrangement index r = 1. We consider arrangement 1 from Table 5.2. This arrangement is {1 2 3 4 5 6}.

Step 2. Construct the processing time matrices of the subsets within arrangement r. The processing time matrices of the subsets {1 2 3} and {4 5 6} within arrangement 1 are:

$$T_{11} = \begin{pmatrix} 6 & 7 & 3 \\ 12 & 2 & 3 \\ 4 & 6 & 8 \end{pmatrix}, \qquad T_{21} = \begin{pmatrix} 3 & 11 & 7 \\ 6 & 8 & 10 \\ 2 & 14 & 12 \end{pmatrix},$$

respectively.

Step 3. Determine the minimum schedule time associated with each subset within arrangement r and find the starting and completion times on all machines. Employing one of the available techniques for solving each subset independently, the optimal sequences and the associated schedule times of subsets 1 and 2 within arrangement 1 are:

Arrangement	Subset 1		Subset 2	
r	S_{1r}	$c^{+}(S_{1r})$	S_{2r}	$c^{+}(S_{2r})$
1	{3 1 2}	27	{6 4 5}	45

The starting and completion times associated with these subsets are:

Machine	Subset 1		Subset 2	
m	s_{11m}	c_{11m}	s_{21m}	c_{21m}
1	0	22	0	11
2	4	24	2	35
3	10	27	16	45

The above results appear on the Gantt charts shown in Figure 5.7.

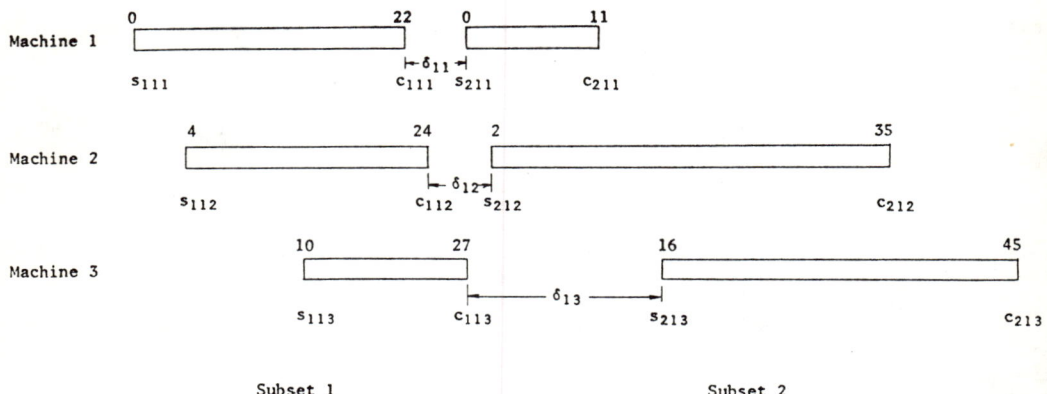

Figure 5.7. Gantt Charts Depicting Two Optimal Sequences within Arrangement 1

Step 4. Compute the idle times between each two successive subsets within arrangement r on all machines such that

$$\delta_{grm} = c^{+}(S_{gr}) - c_{grm} + s_{g+1,rm}, \qquad g = 1, 2, \ldots, G-1,$$
$$m = 1, 2, \ldots, M.$$

Since the first operation in subset 2 starts as soon as the last operation in subset 1 is completed, the idle time on each machine is computed such that

$$\delta_{11m} = c^{+}(S_{11}) - c_{11m} + s_{21m}, \qquad m = 1, 2, 3,$$

or

$$\delta_{111} = 27 - 22 + 0 = 5,$$

$$\delta_{112} = 27 - 24 + 2 = 5,$$

$$\delta_{113} = 27 - 27 + 16 = 16.$$

Thus, the idle times between subsets 1 and 2 on machines 1, 2, and 3 are 5, 5, and 16, respectively, see Figure 5.7.

Step 5. Select the minimum idle time between each two successive subsets within arrangement r such that

$$\Delta_{gr} = \min_{m} \left(\delta_{grm}\right), \qquad g = 1, 2, \ldots, G-1.$$

To avoid overlapping of jobs on any machine, select the minimum idle time such that

$$\Delta_{11} = \min_{m} \left(\delta_{11m}\right),$$

$$= \min \left(5 \quad 5 \quad 16\right) = 5.$$

This allows all operations in subset 2 to start five units of time earlier on all machines without causing any conflict or overlapping of the operations in subset 1.

Step 6. Compute the schedule time overall J jobs in arrangement r such that

$$c^{+}(S_r) = \sum_{g=1}^{G} c^{+}(S_{gr}) - \sum_{g=1}^{G-1} \Delta_{gr}.$$

The schedule time associated with arrangement 1 is

$$c^{+}(S_1) = \sum_{g=1}^{2} c^{+}(S_{g1}) - \Delta_{11}$$

$$= (27 + 45) - 5 = 67.$$

This schedule time is shown in Table 5.2.

Step 7. Increase the arrangement index r by one and repeat steps 2-6 until all the arrangements are evaluated and the corresponding schedule times are obtained. Table 5.2, displays the 20 arrangements and the corresponding schedule times.

Step 8. Observe the minimum schedule time such that

$$c^{+}(S) = \min_{r} \left(c^{+}(S_r)\right).$$

It appears from examining Table 5.2 that the minimum schedule time is 57. This value is the decomposition solution with K = 3.

Decomposition with K = 2. This decomposition solution is obtained by first constructing the complete set of arrangements of 6 jobs involving 3 subsets, each having 2 jobs. The number of such arrangements is R = $6!/(2!)^3$ or 90. The above procedure is followed step by step to obtain the schedule times associated with these arrangements.

For example, the overall schedule time of the first of the 90 arrangements {1 2 3 4 5 6} is computed below. The processing time matrices of subsets 1, 2 and 3 within that arrangement are

$$T_{11} = \begin{pmatrix} 6 & 7 & 3 \\ 12 & 2 & 3 \end{pmatrix}, \quad T_{21} = \begin{pmatrix} 4 & 6 & 8 \\ 3 & 11 & 7 \end{pmatrix}, \quad T_{31} = \begin{pmatrix} 6 & 8 & 10 \\ 2 & 14 & 12 \end{pmatrix}.$$

The optimal sequences and the associated schedule times for the subsets within arrangement 1 are:

Arrangement r	Subset 1 S_{1r}	$c^+(S_{1r})$	Subset 2 S_{2r}	$c^+(S_{2r})$	Subset 3 S_{3r}	$c^+(S_{3r})$
1	{1 2}	23	{3 4}	28	{6 5}	38

The starting and completion times for the above subsets on machines 1, 2 and 3 are:

Machine m	Subset 1 s_{11m}	c_{11m}	Subset 2 s_{21m}	c_{21m}	Subset 3 s_{31m}	c_{31m}
1	0	18	0	7	0	8
2	6	20	4	21	2	24
3	13	23	10	28	16	38

The idle times between subsets 1 and 2 are computed on all machines such that

$$\delta_{11m} = c^+(S_{11}) - c_{11m} + s_{21m}, \quad m = 1, 2, 3,$$

or

$$\delta_{111} = 23 - 18 + 0 = 5,$$

$$\delta_{112} = 23 - 20 + 4 = 7,$$

$$\delta_{113} = 23 - 23 + 10 = 10.$$

Similarly, the idle times between subsets 2 and 3 are

$$\delta_{21m} = c^+(S_{21}) - c_{21m} + s_{21m}, \quad m = 1, 2, 3,$$

or

$$\delta_{211} = 28 - 7 + 0 = 21,$$

$$\delta_{212} = 28 - 21 + 2 = 9,$$

$$\delta_{213} = 28 - 28 + 16 = 16.$$

The Gantt Charts appearing in Figure 5.8, show the idle times between each of the two successive subsets on each machine. The minimum idle time between subsets 1 and 2 is

$$\Delta_{11} = \min (5\ 7\ 10) = 5,$$

and that between subsets 2 and 3 is

$$\Delta_{21} = \min (21\ 9\ 16) = 9.$$

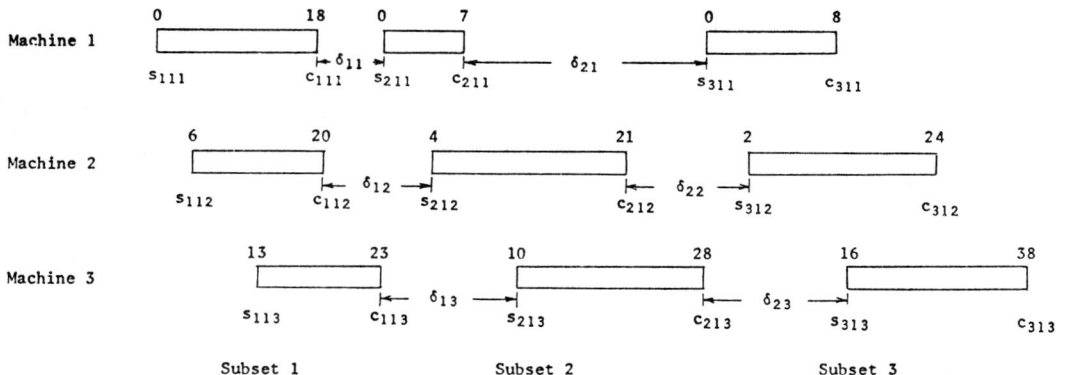

Figure 5.8. Gantt Charts Depicting Three Optimal Sequences within Arrangement 1

Therefore, the schedule time of the combined subsets within arrangement 1 is computed such that

$$c^+(S_1) = \sum_{g=1}^{3} c^+(S_{g1}) - \sum_{g=1}^{2} \Delta_{g1},$$

$$= (23 + 28 + 38) - (5 + 9) = 75.$$

Proceeding as above, the schedule times of the remaining arrangements are obtained. These schedule times are ordered and the minimum value of 57 is observed. This value is the decomposition solution with K = 2. The frequency of the distinct schedule times is displayed in Table 5.3.

Table 5.3 Frequency Table of Schedule Times Obtained by Decomposition

Schedule Time	Decomposition with K = 1	Decomposition with K = 2	Decomposition with K = 3	Decomposition with K = 6
57	3	1	1	1
59	92	1	2	
60	37	6	3	
61	37	2	3	
62	41	6	4	
63	50	12	1	
64	60	16	2	
65	45	4	1	
66	45	3		
67	59	6	3	
68	51	15		
69	31	5		
70	24	1		
71	29	5		
72	31	1		
73	21	3		
74	22	1		
75	7	1		
76	24	1		
77	3			
78	6			
80	2			
	720	90	20	1

Decomposition with K = 1. This decomposition solution is found by first constructing the complete set of arrangements of 6 jobs involving 6 subsets, each having one job. The number of such arrangements is $R = 6!/(1!)^6$ or 720. Note that these arrangements are exactly the 720 sequences obtained by complete enumeration in the preceding section. The sequences are evaluated to determine the corresponding schedule times. These schedule times are ordered and the frequencies of the distinct schedule times are shown in Table 5.3. The minimum schedule time is 57. For convenience, this will be referred to as the decomposition solution with K = 1.

The distinct schedule times obtained by decomposition with K = 1, 2, 3, and 6 are tabulated in ascending order and the corresponding frequencies displayed in

Table 5.3. For comparison, several statistics are computed and shown in Table 5.4. In examining the results in Tables 5.3 and 5.4, we observe the following: (1) the number of distinct schedule times is much less than the number of arrangements evaluated; (2) the distinct schedule times have lower frequencies of occurrence as K increases; (3) all decomposition solutions of this problem are optimal; (4) the spread of schedule times (that is, the difference between the longest and shortest schedules times) becomes narrower as the number of jobs in each subset increases; (5) the mean schedule time is shifted toward the optimal value as K increases; and (6) as a direct consequence of the narrower spread of the distribution as K increases, the variance of schedule time decreases.

Table 5.4. Comparative Data of Various Decomposition Solutions

Statistics	Decomposition with K=1	Decomposition with K=2	Decomposition with K=3
Number of arrangements	720	90	20
Number of distinct schedule times	22	19	9
Mean of schedule times	65.84	65.73	62.15
Variance of schedule times	25.27	15.07	7.92
Minimum schedule time	57.00	57.00	57.00
Maximum schedule time	80.00	76.00	67.00

In order to generalize the above observations and obtain conclusive results, considerable experimentation has been conducted by Ashour [1,3]. The number of flow- and job-shop problems investigated is 128 selected with 6 to 40 jobs and 3 to 10 machines. The processing times of jobs on machines are generated at random from a uniform distribution with various intervals. The decomposition solutions with $K = 1$ are obtained for flow-shop problems having up to six jobs by constructing a complete set of schedules (complete enumeration). For flow-shop problems consisting of more than six jobs and job-shop problems of any size, a subset is randomly generated from the set of all schedules (partial enumeration). However, the decomposition solutions with $1 < K < J$ are obtained for problems having up to eight jobs by constructing a complete set of arrangements of J jobs involving G subsets, each having K jobs (complete enumeration). For problems having more than eight jobs, a subset is generated at random from the set of all arrangements (partial enumeration).

The partial enumeration solution is obtained by sampling with replacement, which is more convenient on the computer, and evaluating a certain number of sequences. The number of sequences n is selected so that there is at least a specified probability α, that at least one of the sequences will lie in the portion p of the schedule time distribution. Thus, the probability of obtaining the minimum schedule time is

$$1 - (1 - p)^n \geq \alpha .$$

With a selection of p as 0.001 and a probability of (1 - α) or 0.95 of obtaining the minimum schedule time, the sample size n is approximately 3000 sequences. In reviewing the relative frequencies of the minimum schedule times in all problems solved by complete enumeration the range of p obtained is from 0.001 to 0.039. This supports the selection of the value of p. Since the partial enumeration does not guarantee optimality, an estimate of the minimum schedule time is computed as in Section 4.2.

For comparison, the quality of the decomposition solutions with $1 < K < J$ is investigated. The quality of solution, referred to as the relative efficiency, is defined as the quotient of the optimal solution and the decomposition solution. The Matched-Pairs t test is used to test the conjecture that the mean of the schedule times shifts toward the minimum as the number of jobs in each subset increases. Furthermore, the computer times spent to obtain the various solutions are compared. Rather than make a complete report of all experiments conducted in this study, we shall limit our discussion to one experiment and then enumerate the most significant results obtained from all experiments. The reader who is interested in other experiments is referred to Ashour [3], however.

One of the experiments in this study consists of 100 flow-shop problems, each of which has 6 jobs and 3 machines. The processing times are generated from a uniform distribution with the interval [1,30], inclusive. The decomposition results with different K's are obtained, as in the above sample problem, and summarized.

To observe the statistical distributions of both the minimum schedule times and the mean schedule times, the corresponding relative cumulative frequencies are plotted on normal probability papers as shown in Figures 5.9 and 5.10, respectively. It should be pointed out that a straight line appearance of the sample cumulative

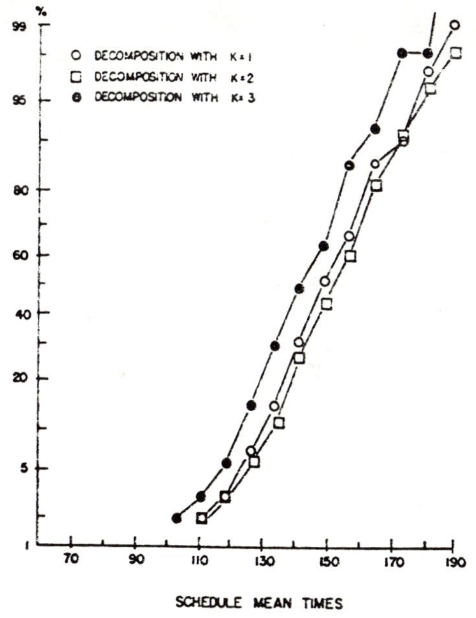

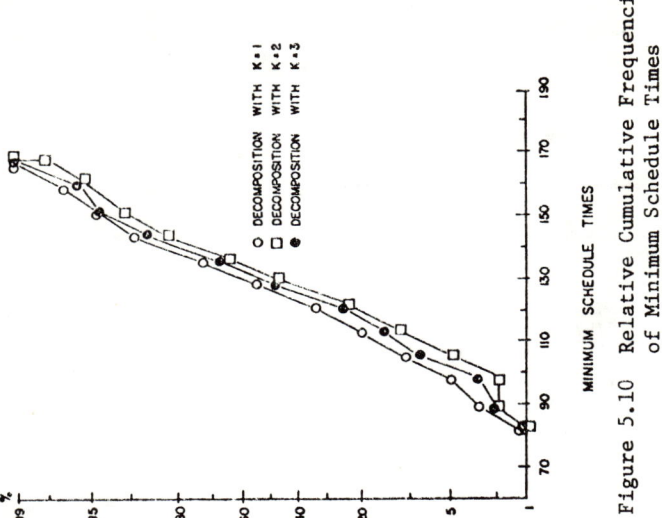

Figure 5.10 Relative Cumulative Frequencies of Minimum Schedule Times

Figure 5.9 Relative Cumulative Frequencies of Mean Schedule Times

function indicates a resemblance to a normal distribution. The sample means and standard deviation of the minimum schedule times and mean schedule times are shown below:

Statistics	Decomposition With K = 1	Decomposition With K = 2	Decomposition With K = 3
Minimum Schedule Times			
Sample Mean	127.14	131.37	129.54
Sample Standard Deviation	17.02	16.51	16.76
Mean Schedule Times			
Sample Mean	151.22	153.65	143.98
Sample Standard Deviation	16.97	17.08	16.91

The examination of Figure 5.9 reveals that decomposition with K = 3 yields minimum values closer to the optimal than decomposition with K = 2. Figure 5.10 shows that the mean values obtained by decomposition with K = 3 seems to be shifted toward the optimal. This is not the case for decomposition with K = 2, however. These results are supported by applying the Matched-Pairs t test. To compare the quality of decomposition solutions with $1 < K < J$ with the optimal values, the relative efficiencies are computed and tabulated in Table 5.5. This table shows that both decomposition with K = 2 and K = 3 produce 21 and 43 optimal solutions, respectively, out of 100. The results show also that 92 decomposition solutions with K = 3 have efficiencies greater than or equal to 0.95; however, those with K = 2 are only 79.

Essentially the same results seem to hold for any problem size. Therefore the most significant results of all computational experiments can be summarized as follows:

1. The decomposition procedure reduces the problem of construction and evaluating sequences to a limited number of arrangements. The number of these arrangements decreases as the number of jobs in each subset increases. For example, in a flow-shop problem of six jobs, the number of all sequences is 6! or 720; however, there are 90 arrangements of six jobs involving three subsets each having two jobs. The number of arrangements is reduced to 20 when the number of jobs in each subset is three.

Table 5.5 Efficiencies of Decomposition Solutions

Efficiency	Decomposition with K=1	Decomposition with K=2	Decomposition with K=3	Decomposition with K=G
1.00	100	21	43	100
0.99		12	19	
0.98		16	9	
0.97		10	10	
0.96		8	6	
0.95		12	5	
0.94		6	2	
0.93		6	1	
0.92		5	1	
0.91		1	1	
0.90		2	1	
0.89				
0.88			1	
0.87				
0.86			1	
0.85				
0.84				
0.83	___	1	___	___
	100	100	100	100

2. The number of distinct schedule times is much less than the number of arrangements evaluated. For example, in our sample problem, the distinct schedule times obtained by decomposition with K = 1, 2, and 3 are 22, 19 and 9, respectively. However, the arrangements from which those are obtained are 720, 90 and 20, respectively.

3. The distinct schedule times have lower frequencies of occurrence as the number of jobs in each subset increases. Therefore, decomposition with 1< K < J reduces the redundancies of the sequences. In general, the number of these redundancies decreases as the number of jobs in each subset increases.

4. The spread of schedule times becomes narrower as the number of jobs in each subset increases. For example, the sample problem shows that the sample ranges of decomposition distributions with K = 1, 2, and 3 are 57 to 80, 57 to 76, and 57 to 67, respectively. In the case of decomposition with K = 6, the distribution is degenerate. The explanation for this is two-fold. First, in obtaining the schedule times overall jobs by decomposition, the minimum schedule times are combined within each arrangement. Second, in combining these schedule times there are idle times on

the machines between each two successive subsets within each arrangement. The amount of the total idle time in each arrangement decreases and hence, the combined schedule time becomes shorter with the decrease in the number of subsets.

5. The decomposition solutions with $1 < K < J$ are improved as the number of jobs in each subset increases. For example, different solutions have been obtained for a (40x3) flow-shop problem. The decomposition solutions with $K = 8$, 10, and 20 are 189, 185, and 180. The decomposition solution with $K = 1$ obtained by sampling from the corresponding distribution is 181. A lower bound on the schedule time is found to be 179.

6. The relative frequency of the shortest schedule time increases as the number of jobs in each subset increases. For example, different solutions have been obtained for a (12x4) flow-shop problem. The probability of obtaining a solution by decomposition with $K = 1$, 3, 4, and 6 is .0007, .001, .002 and .01, respectively.

7. The mean of the schedules times, in general, shifts toward the optimal as the number of jobs in each subset increases except in those decomposition cases in which the values of K are very close to one. Such cases are not sensitive to shift toward the optimal.

8. The variance of the schedule times decreases as the number of jobs in each subset increases. This indicates that most of the schedule times concentrate heavily about the mean as the number of jobs in each subset increases. This result is a direct consequence of the spread of decomposition distributions. For example, in our sample problem, the variances of the decomposition solutions with $K = 1$, 2, and 3 are 25.27, 15.07, and 7.92, respectively.

9. The decomposition with $1 < K < J$ produces at least a good solution. In this investigation, 245 decomposition solutions with $1 < K < J$ are obtained. These solutions yield between 0.83 and 1.03 efficiencies. Five solutions have efficiencies less than 0.90. Approximately 86 per cent yield efficiencies equal to or greater than 0.95 and about 34 per cent are optimal.

10. The computer time required to obtain the decomposition solution with $K = J/2$ is less than that required to obtain any other solution. Moreover, the computer time

Table 5.6 Comparative Results Obtained By Original And Modified Decomposition Procedures

Experiment No.	Problem Size	No. of Problems	Modified Decomposition Procedure					Original Decomposition Procedure				
			Computer Time (seconds) IBM 360/50		Efficiency		Computer Time (seconds) IBM 360/50		Efficiency	
			Range	Mean	Range	Mean	Range	Mean	Range	Mean
I	(6x3)	100	3.11 - 3.92	3.16	0.88 - 1.00	0.96	44.72 - 48.48	47.36	0.86 - 1.00	0.94
II	(6x4)	50	3.25 - 3.74	3.52	0.80 - 1.00	0.94	51.83 - 54.91	52.88	0.87 - 1.00	0.92
III	(6x5)	50	4.15 - 4.68	4.17	0.81 - 0.99	0.93	59.40 - 65.52	62.36	0.94 - 1.00	0.92
IV	(7x3)	50	15.19 - 17.25	15.62	0.85 - 1.00	0.94	149.38 - 156.72	151.38	0.86 - 1.00	0.94
V	(7x4)	50	28.18 - 29.79	28.30	0.84 - 1.00	0.92	160.32 - 169.44	163.42	0.87 - 1.00	0.92
VI	(7x5)	50	23.83 - 24.92	24.21	0.72 - 1.00	0.92	168.98 - 173.82	169.97	0.79 - 1.00	0.92
VII	(8x3)	50	16.63 - 17.18	16.77	0.88 - 1.00	0.96	195.72 - 201.68	198.92	0.91 - 1.00	0.97
VIII	(8x4)	50	20.19 - 21.85	20.37	0.87 - 0.99	0.93	205.13 - 210.18	208.29	0.90 - 1.00	0.93
IX	(8x5)	50	27.15 - 27.90	27.62	0.84 - 0.97	0.92	220.24 - 227.82	223.39	0.87 - 1.00	0.91
X	(10x3)	25	20.85 - 21.79	21.38	0.78 - 1.00	0.94	501.28 - 512.72	506.64	0.83 - 1.00	0.93
XI	(12x3)	25	37.82 - 38.89	38.16	0.89 - 1.00	0.96	1363.64 - 1416.88	1378.80	0.92 - 1.00	0.94

required to obtain the decomposition solution with $1 < K < J$ increases as the number of jobs in each subset decreases.

In conclusion, the above results suggest that the distribution of decomposition with $K = J/2$ is preferable to the others. This conclusion has led us to modify the above procedure in order to extend the computational feasibility of the existing techniques for solving the subsets within each arrangement [4]. This has been accomplished by constructing only the first $R/2$ arrangements, since any arrangement r is equivalent to arrangement $R - r + 1$, where $r = 1, 2, ..., R/2$. By equivalent arrangements we mean that subsets 1 and 2, within arrangement r, consist of the same jobs as those in subsets 2 and 1 within arrangement $R - r + 1$, respectively. For example, Table 5.2 shows that arrangements 1, 2, ..., 9, and 10 are equivalent to arrangements 20, 19, ..., 12, and 11, respectively. It is then sufficient to find the minimum schedule time of each of the two subsets within each of the $R/2$ arrangements. The overall schedule times associated with the equivalent arrangement $R - r + 1$ is obtained by switching the sequences yielding the minimum values of both subsets within arrangement r. This reduces the computational effort involved.

Table 5.6 displays the efficiency of solutions and the computational time obtained by both decomposition procedures. Two conclusions can be made. First, the computational time required to obtain the solution by the modified decomposition is reduced immensely. This has been achieved through improving the partitioning and combining phases in addition to the use of an efficient procedure such as the branch-and-bound technique. Second, there are no significant differences between both efficiencies; however, the efficiencies, in general, are high; the mean efficiency ranges between 0.91 and 0.97.

This chapter completes the study of the fundamental concepts of the shop scheduling problem. The study has been presented in such a way that the reader fully appreciates the complexity that faces further progress in the analysis of this problem.

REFERENCES

[1] Ashour, S., "A Decomposition Approach for the Machine Scheduling Problem," *The International Journal of Production Research*, Vol. 6, No. 2, 1967, pp. 109-122.

[2] Ashour, S., "A Procedure for Finding an Economical Solution to Machine Scheduling Problems," presented before the Operations Research Around the World Meeting, Tokyo-Kyoto, Japan, August 14-17, 1967.

[3] Ashour, S., "A Statistical Analysis of Production Scheduling Systems," *Journal of Operations Research Society of Japan*, Vol. 12, No. 2, 1970, pp. 65-86.

[4] Ashour, S., "A Modified Decomposition Algorithm for Scheduling Problems," *The International Journal of Production Research*, Vol. 8, No. 3, 1970, pp. 281-284.

[5] Conway, R. W., W. L. Maxwell and L. W. Miller, *Theory of Scheduling*, Addison-Wesley Publishing Company, Reading, Massachusetts, 1967, pp. 100-102.

[6] Elmaghraby, S. E., "The Machine Sequencing Problem - Review and Extensions," *Naval Research Logistics Quarterly*, Vol. 15, No. 2, 1968, pp. 205-232.

[7] Fisher, H. and G. L. Thompson, "Probabilistic Learning Combinations of Local Job-Shop Scheduling Rules," Chapter 15 in *Industrial Scheduling*, (eds. J. F. Muth and G. L. Thompson), Prentice-Hall Inc., Englewood Cliffs, New Jersey, 1963.

[8] Giffler, B. and G. L. Thompson, "Algorithms for Solving Production Scheduling Problems," *Operations Research*, Vol. 8, No. 4, 1960, pp. 487-503.

[9] Giffler, B., G. L. Thompson and V. VanNess, "Numerical Experience with Linear and Monte Carlo Algorithms for Solving Production Scheduling Problems," Chapter 3 in *Industrial Scheduling*, (eds. J. F. Muth and G. L. Thompson), Prentice-Hall Inc., Englewood Cliffs, New Jersey, 1963.

[10] Heller, J., "Combinatorial, Probabilistic and Statistical Aspects of an M x J Scheduling Problem," Report NYO-2540, Atomic Energy Commission Computed and Applied Mathematics Center, Institute of Mathematical Science, New York University, New York, February 1959.

[11] Heller, J., "Combinatorial Properties of Machine Shop Scheduling," Report NYO-2879, Atomic Energy Commission Computed and Applied Mathematics Center, Institute of Mathematical Science, New York University, New York, July 1959.

[12] Heller, J., "Some Numerical Experiments for an M x J Flow Shop and its Decision-Theoretical Aspects," *Operations Research*, Vol. 8, No. 2, 1960, pp. 178-184.

[13] Heller, J. and G. Logemann, "An Algorithm for the Construction and Evaluation of Feasible Schedules," *Management Science*, Vol. 8, No. 2, 1962, pp. 168-183.

[14] Nugent, C. E., "On Sampling Approaches to the Solution of n-by-m Static Sequencing Problem," Ph.D. Thesis, Cornell University, Ithaca, New York, 1964.

Lecture Notes in Economics and Mathematical Systems

(Vol. 1–15: Lecture Notes in Operations Research and Mathematical Economics, Vol. 16–59: Lecture Notes in Operations Research and Mathematical Systems)

Vol. 1: H. Bühlmann, H. Loeffel, E. Nievergelt, Einführung in die Theorie und Praxis der Entscheidung bei Unsicherheit. 2. Auflage, IV, 125 Seiten 4°. 1969. DM 16,–

Vol. 2: U. N. Bhat, A Study of the Queueing Systems M/G/1 and GI/M/1. VIII, 78 pages. 4°. 1968. DM 16,–

Vol. 3: A. Strauss, An Introduction to Optimal Control Theory. VI, 153 pages. 4°. 1968. DM 16,–

Vol. 4: Einführung in die Methode Branch and Bound. Herausgegeben von F. Weinberg. VIII, 159 Seiten. 4°. 1968. DM 16,–

Vol. 5: Hyvärinen, Information Theory for Systems Engineers. VIII, 205 pages. 4°. 1968. DM 16,–

Vol. 6: H. P. Künzi, O. Müller, E. Nievergelt, Einführungskursus in die dynamische Programmierung. IV, 103 Seiten. 4°. 1968. DM 16,–

Vol. 7: W. Popp, Einführung in die Theorie der Lagerhaltung. VI, 173 Seiten. 4°. 1968. DM 16,–

Vol. 8: J. Teghem, J. Loris-Teghem, J. P. Lambotte, Modèles d'Attente M/G/1 et GI/M/1 à Arrivées et Services en Groupes. IV, 53 pages. 4°. 1969. DM 16,–

Vol. 9: E. Schultze, Einführung in die mathematischen Grundlagen der Informationstheorie. VI, 116 Seiten. 4°. 1969. DM 16,–

Vol. 10: D. Hochstädter, Stochastische Lagerhaltungsmodelle. VI, 269 Seiten. 4°. 1969. DM 18,–

Vol. 11/12: Mathematical Systems Theory and Economics. Edited by H. W. Kuhn and G. P. Szegö. VIII, IV, 486 pages. 4°. 1969. DM 34,–

Vol. 13: Heuristische Planungsmethoden. Herausgegeben von F. Weinberg und C. A. Zehnder. II, 93 Seiten. 4°. 1969. DM 16,–

Vol. 14: Computing Methods in Optimization Problems. Edited by A. V. Balakrishnan. V, 191 pages. 4°. 1969. DM 16,–

Vol. 15: Economic Models, Estimation and Risk Programming: Essays in Honor of Gerhard Tintner. Edited by K. A. Fox, G. V. L. Narasimham and J. K. Sengupta. VIII, 461 pages. 4°. 1969. DM 24,–

Vol. 16: H. P. Künzi und W. Oettli, Nichtlineare Optimierung: Neuere Verfahren, Bibliographie. IV, 180 Seiten. 4°. 1969. DM 16,–

Vol. 17: H. Bauer und K. Neumann, Berechnung optimaler Steuerungen, Maximumprinzip und dynamische Optimierung. VIII, 188 Seiten. 4°. 1969. DM 16,–

Vol. 18: M. Wolff, Optimale Instandhaltungspolitiken in einfachen Systemen. V, 143 Seiten. 4°. 1970. DM 16,–

Vol. 19: L. Hyvärinen, Mathematical Modeling for Industrial Processes. VI, 122 pages. 4°. 1970. DM 16,–

Vol. 20: G. Uebe, Optimale Fahrpläne. IX, 161 Seiten. 4°. 1970. DM 16,–

Vol. 21: Th. Liebling, Graphentheorie in Planungs- und Tourenproblemen am Beispiel des städtischen Straßendienstes. IX, 118 Seiten. 4°. 1970. DM 16,–

Vol. 22: W. Eichhorn, Theorie der homogenen Produktionsfunktion. VIII, 119 Seiten. 4°. 1970. DM 16,–

Vol. 23: A. Ghosal, Some Aspects of Queueing and Storage Systems. IV, 93 pages. 4°. 1970. DM 16,–

Vol. 24: Feichtinger, Lernprozesse in stochastischen Automaten. V, 66 Seiten. 4°. 1970. DM 16,–

Vol. 25: R. Henn und O. Opitz, Konsum- und Produktionstheorie. I. II, 124 Seiten. 4°. 1970. DM 16,–

Vol. 26: D. Hochstädter und G. Uebe, Ökonometrische Methoden. XII, 250 Seiten. 4°. 1970. DM 18,–

Vol. 27: I. H. Mufti, Computational Methods in Optimal Control Problems. IV, 45 pages. 4°. 1970. DM 16,–

Vol. 28: Theoretical Approaches to Non-Numerical Problem Solving. Edited by R. B. Banerji and M. D. Mesarovic. VI, 466 pages. 4°. 1970. DM 24,–

Vol. 29: S. E. Elmaghraby, Some Network Models in Management Science. III, 177 pages. 4°. 1970. DM 16,–

Vol. 30: H. Noltemeier, Sensitivitätsanalyse bei diskreten linearen Optimierungsproblemen. VI, 102 Seiten. 4°. 1970. DM 16,–

Vol. 31: M. Kühlmeyer, Die nichtzentrale t-Verteilung. II, 106 Seiten. 4°. 1970. DM 16,–

Vol. 32: F. Bartholomes und G. Hotz, Homomorphismen und Reduktionen linearer Sprachen. XII, 143 Seiten. 4°. 1970. DM 16,–

Vol. 33: K. Hinderer, Foundations of Non-stationary Dynamic Programming with Discrete Time Parameter. VI, 160 pages. 4°. 1970. DM 16,–

Vol. 34: H. Störmer, Semi-Markoff-Prozesse mit endlich vielen Zuständen. Theorie und Anwendungen. VII, 128 Seiten. 4°. 1970. DM 16,–

Vol. 35: F. Ferschl, Markovketten. VI, 168 Seiten. 4°. 1970. DM 16,–

Vol. 36: M. P. J. Magill, On a General Economic Theory of Motion. VI, 95 pages. 4°. 1970. DM 16,–

Vol. 37: H. Müller-Merbach, On Round-Off Errors in Linear Programming. VI, 48 pages. 4°. 1970. DM 16,–

Vol. 38: Statistische Methoden I, herausgegeben von E. Walter. VIII, 338 Seiten. 4°. 1970. DM 22,–

Vol. 39: Statistische Methoden II, herausgegeben von E. Walter. IV, 155 Seiten. 4°. 1970. DM 16,–

Vol. 40: H. Drygas, The Coordinate-Free Approach to Gauss-Markov Estimation. VIII, 113 pages. 4°. 1970. DM 16,–

Vol. 41: U. Ueing, Zwei Lösungsmethoden für nichtkonvexe Programmierungsprobleme. VI, 92 Seiten. 4°. 1971. DM 16,–

Vol. 42: A. V. Balakrishnan, Introduction to Optimization Theory in a Hilbert Space. IV, 153 pages. 4°. 1971. DM 16,–

Vol. 43: J. A. Morales, Bayesian Full Information Structural Analysis. VI, 154 pages. 4°. 1971. DM 16,–

Vol. 44: G. Feichtinger, Stochastische Modelle demographischer Prozesse. XIII, 404 pages. 4°. 1971. DM 28,–

Vol. 45: K. Wendler, Hauptaustauschschritte (Principal Pivoting). II, 64 pages. 4°. 1971. DM 16,–

Vol. 46: C. Boucher, Leçons sur la théorie des automates mathématiques. VIII, 193 pages. 4°. 1971. DM 18,–

Vol. 47: H. A. Nour Eldin, Optimierung linearer Regelsysteme mit quadratischer Zielfunktion. VIII, 163 pages. 4°. 1971. DM 16,–

Vol. 48: M. Constam, Fortran für Anfänger. VI, 143 pages. 4°. 1971. DM 16,–

Vol. 49: Ch. Schneeweiß, Regelungstechnische stochastische Optimierungsverfahren. XI, 254 pages. 4°. 1971. DM 16,–

Vol. 50: Unternehmensforschung Heute – Übersichtsvorträge der Züricher Tagung von SVOR und DGU, September 1970. Herausgegeben von M. Beckmann. VI, 133 pages. 4°. 1971. DM 16,–

Vol. 51: Digitale Simulation. Herausgegeben von K. Bauknecht und W. Nef. IV, 207 pages. 4°. 1971. DM 18,–

Vol. 52: Invariant Imbedding. Proceedings of the Summer Workshop on Invariant Imbedding Held at the University of Southern California, June – August 1970. Edited by R. E. Bellman and E. D. Denman. IV, 148 pages. 4°. 1971. DM 16,–

Vol. 53: J. Rosenmüller, Kooperative Spiele und Märkte. IV, 152 pages. 4°. 1971. DM 16,–

Vol. 54: C. C. von Weizsäcker, Steady State Capital Theory. III, 102 pages. 4°. 1971. DM 16,–

Vol. 55: P. A. V. B. Swamy, Statistical Inference in Random Coefficient Regression Models. VIII, 209 pages. 4°. 1971. DM 20,–

Vol. 56: Mohamed A. El-Hodiri, Constrained Extrema. Introduction to the Differentiable Case with Economic Applications. III, 130 pages. 4°. 1971. DM 16,–

Vol. 57: E. Freund, Zeitvariable Mehrgrößensysteme. VII, 160 pages. 4°. 1971. DM 16,–

Vol. 58: P. B. Hagelschuer, Theorie der linearen Dekomposition. VII, 191 pages. 4°.1971. DM 18,–

Vol. 59: J. A. Hanson, Growth in Open Economics. IV, 127 pages. 4°. 1971. DM 16,–

Vol. 60: H. Hauptmann, Schätz- und Kontrolltheorie in stetigen dynamischen Wirtschaftsmodellen. V, 104 pages. 4°. 1971. DM 16,–

Vol. 61: K. H. F. Meyer, Wartesysteme mit variabler Bearbeitungsrate. VII, 314 pages. 4°. 1971. DM 24,–

Vol. 62: W. Krelle u. G. Gabisch unter Mitarbeit von J. Burgermeister, Wachstumstheorie. VII, 223 pages. 4°. 1972. DM 20,–

Vol. 63: J. Kohlas, Monte Carlo Simulation im Operations Research. VI, 162 pages. 4°. 1972. DM 16,–

Vol. 64: P. Gessner u. K. Spremann, Optimierung in Funktionenräumen. IV, 120 pages. 4°. 1972. DM 16,–.

Vol. 65: W. Everling, Exercises in Computer Systems Analysis. VIII, 184 pages. 4°. 1972. DM 16,–

Vol. 66: F. Bauer, P. Garabedian und D. Korn, Supercritical Wing Sections. V, 211 pages. 4°. 1972. DM 20,–

Vol. 67: I. V. Girsanov, Lectures on Mathematical Theory of Extremum Problems. V, 136 pages. 4°. 1972. DM 16,–

Vol. 68: J. Loeckx, Computability and Decidability. An Introduction for Students of Computer Science. VI, 76 pages. 4°. 1972. DM 16,–

Vol. 69: S. Ashour, Sequencing Theory. V, 133 pages. 4°. 1972. DM 16,–.